MODERN AMERICA AND ANCIENT ROME

MODERN AMERICA AND ANCIENT ROME

—

AN ESSAY IN HISTORICAL COMPARISON AND ANALOGY

Simon Kiessling de Courcy

Algora Publishing
New York

Library of Congress Cataloging-in-Publication Data —

Names: DeCourcy, Simon Kiessling, 1971-
Title: Modern America and ancient Rome: an essay in historical comparison
    and analogy / Simon Kiessling DeCourcy.
Description: New York: Algora Publishing, 2016. | Includes bibliographical
    references and index.
Identifiers: LCCN 2016001809| ISBN 9781628941531 (soft cover: alkaline
    paper) | ISBN 9781628941548 (hard cover: alkaline paper)
Subjects: LCSH: Rome—Civilization. | Greece—Civilization. | United
    States—Civilization. | Europe—Civilization. | Comparative civilization.
    | Rome—Relations—Greece. | Greece—Relations—Rome. | United
    States—Relations—Europe. | Europe—Relations—United States. | Social
    problems—United States.
Classification: LCC DG78 .D44 2016 | DDC 973—dc23 LC record available at http://
lccn.loc.gov/2016001809

Printed in the United States

TABLE OF CONTENTS

1. Introductory Reflections on the Philosophy of History and Oswald Spengler's Morphological Theory of the High Cultural Formations

As World War I drew to a close in the summer of 1918, the German theorist of history Oswald Spengler published a wide-ranging philosophical treatise on world (or universal) history whose title soon changed into winged words in the heated political atmosphere of the 1920s and 30s. In *The Decline of the West*, Spengler disputed the conventional notion of a linear, universal historical progress extending from the age of antiquity through the Middle Ages to the modern and contemporary world. Instead, he argued that the age of antiquity (i.e., the Greco–Roman era) and the age of the Occident or West (i.e., the European–American period) were in fact two autonomous, essentially self-sufficient historical entities or *high cultures* with axiomatically different concepts of life, time, science, religion, history and art.

Like all the high cultures,[1] Spengler regarded the age of antiquity and the age of the West as two fundamentally independent, self-contained historical formations, each of which is governed by a unique intrinsic logic, has an unmistakably individual view of the world and evolves (or extends) over a certain limited duration of time. History, in this sense, therefore does not constitute one consistent line of universal advancement

---

[1] Overall, Spengler referred to eight high cultures — Babylonian, Egyptian, Chinese, Indian, Mexican, Arabian, Classical and Western — all of which are equal in value and deserve equal recognition.

and progression but rather a *morphological* succession of individual, self-contained, basically unrelated *high cultural formations* that emerge, unfold, mature and decease, one after another, in the course of an all-embracing human history and evolution.

At the same time, Spengler claimed that — in the final analysis — all high cultures follow essentially the same trajectory and structural pattern of historical evolution. Traversing essentially identical cycles of historical development, they pass through the correlating stages of rise, maturation, heyday, decline and demise (or, in the biological terms used and favored by Spengler, of childhood, youth, bloom, old age, petrifaction and death). On this basic supposition, however, the adequate way of relating the history of antiquity with the history of the Occident or West would in fact not be (linear) historical progression but structural analogy and comparison.

Hence, when resorting to the history of antiquity to gain a more profound understanding of Western civilization and its potential destiny and fate, we should not view antiquity as a mere preliminary stage to our own, contemporary context and time but rather as a comprehensively autonomous, self-sufficient historical entity — suitable for comparison and analogy with the history of the West since both formations undergo substantially the same stages of socio-cultural development, follow the same trajectories and are poised to share essentially the same historical fortunes, destinies and fates.

Axiomatically conceiving the high cultural formations as living organisms or creatures, Spengler held that all high cultures ultimately undergo the same biological process of birth, childhood, youth, bloom, old age and death — or, in more specific terms: proceed from feudal beginnings to the cultural and intellectual heyday of a classical period, aged rationalist civilization in a universal, peace-preserving empire (which Spengler generally referred to as the age of Caesarism, i.e., bureaucratic, absolute and universal one-man rule over subjects deprived of any political power, identity and rights), and finally a period of downfall and demise. From this perspective, however, the age of antiquity does not simply represent a preparatory, still imperfect stage of universal human progress but rather a self-contained, essentially autarchic historical formation — having emerged in the eleventh century B.C., flourished in the city-states of ancient Greece, matured in Rome and finally waned in the 5th century

A.D. (while Spengler considered the culture of the Occident or West to have emerged at around A.D. 900, blossomed into a classical period in the age of the European nations and nation states, and turned into a universal, rationalist civilization in the 19th century, culminating in the replacement of European by American predominance since World War I).

Yet like the natural life cycle of biological organisms and living creatures, Spengler argued, the bio-historical development process of the high cultural formations cannot be explained in strictly causal and analytical terms (just as youth cannot be regarded as the cause of age and age cannot be regarded as the cause of death, or the flower regarded as the cause of the fruit). Like the life cycle of living beings, the courses and developments of history as seen by Spengler cannot be *explained* but only *sensed* and *understood*. Similarities and parallels of historical development and evolution among the individual high cultures are hence understandable only to those capable of comprehending a specific, metaphysical "logic of history" which, as Spengler was anxious to point out, differs greatly from the immutable laws of natural science. To study the "comparative morphology of world history" as understood by Spengler thus requires not so much the power of intellectual analysis and causal explanation but rather an innate, compelling sense of historical destiny and fate.

Undoubtedly, many features of Spengler's philosophy of history are highly questionable and greatly influenced by organological patterns and antirationalist narratives of early 20th century thought. Nevertheless, the stimulating potential of Spengler's approach still lies in its capacity, or its promise, to provide indications as to the presumable future course and fate of Western civilization itself. Indeed, Spengler's immodest claim that, on the grounds of his theoretical concept and approach, it had become possible for the first time ever to "predetermine history" and "write a history of the future"[1] rests on the idea that all high cultures inescapably follow the same (structural) trajectory and cycle of historical evolution or, in a narrower sense: that the history of the Occident or West (of Europe and America) is poised to take a similar course and undergo essentially identical stages of development as the history of ancient

---

[1] Oswald Spengler, *Der Untergang des Abendlandes. Umrisse einer Morphologie der Weltgeschichte*, Munich 1963, 3-6 and 152. On 54ss., he goes on to speak of a possible "forward calculation of history."

Greece and Rome. As a consequence thereof, our knowledge of the courses and trajectories of Greco–Roman history raises the prospect and perspective of anticipating the future courses and trajectories of occidental civilization itself — or, to put it in more modest terms: of sharpening our awareness for the potential historical significance of current political, social and cultural phenomena and trends which structurally resemble and correspond to those in the correlating historical stages of ancient Greece and Rome. In the core and final chapter of this essay, I shall therefore discuss the question of what history is capable of telling us about the potential future of Western civilization itself. Can historical analysis and historiographical research (in the sense of comparison and analogy) help us figure out at which point in the life and development cycle of Western civilization we stand at the outset of the 21st century? Which period of ancient history does our own contemporary time most closely resemble or correspond to, and where is history likely to proceed from here? Which trends and challenges of our own, contemporary age should we be watchful of and pay attention to, assuming that the future course of occidental history will bear basic structural resemblance to what happened two thousand years ago in the political and socio-cultural context of ancient Greece and Rome?

In terms of methodology, I will therefore aim to employ Spengler's approach, yet not without maintaining a critical distance: While committed in principle to Spengler's view that the history of antiquity and the history of the West are poised to traverse substantially identical stages of socio-political development and cycles of historical evolution, a key objective of my essay will be to review whether the investigated processes of historical transition, evolution and change can be explained, after all, by analytical, rational and causal means. In this sense, I shall question Spengler's belief that secular historical developments (like the transition to "post heroic" attitudes and values in Hellenistic Greece and postwar Europe, the ultimate submission of Greece and Europe to the Romans and Americans or the seismic changes occurring within the Roman and American republics) cannot be explained in principle on rational and causal grounds but only *sensed* and *understood* as inevitable, fateful symptoms of bio-societal ageing, tiring and exhaustion.

In particular, the questions to be raised within this context will include the following: What caused the rise of post-heroic values, the decline of political ambition, the focus on private aspiration and the preference for individual self-realization in the postclassical ages of ancient Greece and modern Europe respectively? (Chapters 3, 4 and 5) Why do postclassical Greeks and postwar Europeans pin their hopes on pan-Hellenism and pan-Europeanism respectively, while the Romans and Americans remain committed to their inherited national institutions and resolutely oppose universalism or the transfer of sovereign powers to supranational levels and organizations? (Chapter 6) Why did the ancient Greeks consider the Romans as vulgar, boorish and rude in a manner structurally reminiscent of how modern Europeans see the Americans, while the Romans regarded the Greeks as decadent, licentious and weak, structurally reminiscent of how present-day Americans perceive the Europeans? (Chapters 7 and 8) Why do the Romans and Americans remain so ardently committed to religion, while religious indifference, atheism and agnosticism prevail in ancient Greece and modern Europe, and Roman or American prudishness and Puritanism are deplored or ridiculed by the Greeks and Europeans respectively? (Chapter 9) Why do the Romans and Americans so fiercely reject the forces of radical ideology and utopian vision, which thrived and prospered in the postclassical Greek and European worlds? (Chapter 10) What do the shrinking populations of postclassical Greece and Europe have to do with rising levels of geographical mobility and a loss of loyalty to the polis or nation state, whereas the Romans and Americans remain closely tied to their national institutions, ancestral lands and the *spirit of the fields*? (Chapter 11) Why have the Romans and Americans been so reluctant to conquer and annex, refraining for long periods of time from a systematic pursuit of imperial power and the exercise of direct rule over other peoples and nations? (Chapter 12) And finally: Does current American world supremacy show any signs of developing into imperial reign and universal rule, as Roman supremacy of the ancient world did during the second and first century B.C.? Are there any indications of America repeating the fateful trajectory of Rome or, in other words: any signs of political, economic, social and cultural developments within present-day "hegemonic" America which threaten to challenge or tear the fabric of America's republican institutions in a way resembling the (finally lethal) crisis of the Roman republic in the late second and early first century B.C.?

As a matter of course, there have been many attempts already at comparing and analogizing the history of antiquity and the history of the modern world. Often, however, such analogies and comparisons have turned out to be ill-founded, arbitrary or misapplied such as those between Napoleon and Caesar, pax Britannica and pax Romana, Athens and America, World War II and the Second Punic War or, what became very prominent especially since 9/11/2001, between present-day America and Rome's imperial period after the formal establishment of an empire by Augustus in the late first century B.C.[1]

In most of the cases, the failure of comparison and analogy resulted from the fact that the contemplated events, conditions and structures of ancient history did not relate precisely to the same relative stage (or level) of a high culture's life and development cycle as the events, conditions and structures of Western (occidental) history, with which they were compared.[2]

For any comparison and analogy between the age of antiquity and the age of the West to make sense, it therefore appears indispensable — in the first instance — to identify and outline the basic stages or periods of ancient and occidental history and determine which of these stages or periods correspond to each other in the sense of representing the

---

[1] Recent analyses explicitly analogizing present-day America and the ancient Roman Empire include those by Amy Chua, who appreciates the early empire as a charitable, economically successful, religiously pluralistic and racially integrative model of political organization, advising 21st century America to take inspiration from Rome's "Golden Age" in the first century A.D. (Amy Chua, *Day of Empire. How Superpowers Rise to Global Dominance and Why They Fall*, New York 2007); Cullen Murphy, who compares the problems facing present-day America with the problems once having faced imperial Rome — down to analogizing the pressure once exerted by Germanic tribes on the Roman border in the third and fourth century A.D. with today's challenges of illegal immigration from Latin America and the futile efforts to control the American–Mexican border (Cullen Murphy, *Are We Rome? The Fall of an Empire and the Fate of America*, Boston/New York 2008); and Charles Kupchan, who believes that Europe's political integration will eventually challenge the U.S. superpower status, as the EU develops into "an emerging pole, dividing the West into American and European halves," as once was the case when the Roman empire split into a Western and an Eastern half, i.e., the later Byzantium, in the fourth century A.D. (Charles A. Kupchan, *The End of the American Era. U.S. Foreign Policy and the Geopolitics of the Twenty-First Century*, New York 2002, 119/132). For a detailed discussion of America's classification as an *Empire*, cf. Chapter 2.

[2] As we shall see in Chapter 2, even Spengler himself was not immune from establishing false analogies, especially when considering himself the prophet and intellectual champion of a prospective German (or Prussian) Caesar.

---

same levels of development, evolution and progression in the life cycle of the two historical formations. Before seeking for possible lessons and conclusions to be drawn from history for a better understanding of our own, contemporary age and its potential future, we must therefore first identify and analyze the fundamental, concurrent (or correlating) stages of historical development within the ancient, Greco–Roman context and the modern, European–American world.

2. The Four Basic Stages of Ancient and Occidental History

After a preliminary period of feudal rule and socio-cultural maturation, four basic stages of historical development and evolution can be identified in the history of antiquity and in the history of the Occident or West: first, a classical period of the city-states in ancient Greece, i.e., the heyday of the Greek polis and Greek philosophy, drama and art in the 6th and 5th centuries B.C., and of occidental politics and culture in the age of the European nations and nation states. (Those were the times of Athens and Britain, the Spartans and the Prussians, Descartes and Pythagoras, Socrates and Kant.) Both cases were periods of great cultural and intellectual achievement, setting standards for the centuries to come, but they were also times of almost permanent war in a culture of heroism and belligerence where bravery and unconditional loyalty to the city or nation state were regarded as the cardinal virtues, and death as a defender of the polis or nation promised eternal posthumous fame. As the very survival of the city or nation state depended on the willingness of citizens to risk their lives in battle and war, the individual was faced with comprehensive requirements to serve the state in politics, the administration and, most importantly, as a citizen-soldier.

In the later stages of the classical periods in ancient Greece and modern Europe, dynamic processes of change unfolded, in the course of which social barriers were dismantled, constraints to economic freedom removed, and suffrage extended to the middle and lower classes (tradesmen, artisans, peasants and finally laborers), as monarchy or aristocracy gave way to progressive democratization of the municipal or national bodies politic. At the same time, traditional moral values and religious concepts were questioned and transgressed by Socrates and the sophists in ancient Greece, and by enlightenment and the philosophy of life (represented most prominently by Nietzsche) in modern Europe. Eventually, the inner tensions, energies and dynamic potentials building and accumulating in the Greek and European worlds in the late stages of their classical periods erupted, turned expansionist, began overrunning territorial boundaries and emanated to the outside world, thus setting the stage for the second phase in the history of antiquity and in the history of the West.

The beginning of the second stage of historical development, i.e., the postclassical ages of Greece and Europe respectively, was marked by a violent expansion of Greek and European power, as a result of which the small political entities were replaced with large, monarchical and imperialist conglomerations. In ancient Greece, Alexander the Great carried Greek power, commerce and culture to the furthermost points of the world, while the city-states of Athens and Sparta were eclipsed by Macedonia and, later, by the kingdoms of the *diadochi* established after Alexander's death in 323 B.C. In world history terms, Alexander's advent marked the beginning of the age of *Hellenism*, where Greek language and culture extended to the Orient from Persia to the Ganges, the Hindu Kush and the Nile, and Greeks became the ruling elites of Syria, Egypt, Pergamum and the other, smaller kingdoms of the Hellenistic world. In Europe, the first expansionary eruption came with Napoleon in the early 19th century, before advanced industrial capitalism (with its search for new markets for abundant goods production, its scramble for raw material resources and its need for capital exportation) started transgressing national boundaries, and high imperialism undermined the established institutions of the nation state.

Just as Greeks became the socio-cultural and governing elite, and Greek language, architecture, philosophy and education spread to large parts of the civilized world including Persia, Egypt and parts of India in the Hellenistic age, the imperialist powers of 19th century Europe created colonies or *spheres of influence* establishing Europeans as the ruling colonial elite in the military, the economy and the administration, and asserting European lifestyles, technology, manners and thought as the benchmark standards in wide sections of the politically, economically and militarily relevant world. (This subjection of foreign countries and nations must be distinguished from the original Greek and European colonialism of the 8th and 7th century B.C. and the 17th and 18th century A.D., when Greek settlers founded new city states around the Mediterranean such as Miletus or Syracuse, and Europeans settled, for instance, in America, Canada or Australia.)

In fact, the expansionary eras of Greece and Europe respectively were driven by the same boundless expansionary urge and unwillingness to accept limits or constraints. True to his guiding principle that the gods had set no limit to the human being's urge for the extraordinary, Alexander the Great did not content himself with conquering the Persian Empire; he was rather making plans already for further, limitless campaigns of conquest to the Ganges, Arabia, Italy and Carthage, driven by a determination to acquire world supremacy and reach the geographical endpoints of the earth. For Alexander, the traditional boundaries of Greek political thought — such as the divide between Asia and Greece, any transgression of which had long been regarded as a symptom of immoderateness and hubris — no longer required observation. As the Greco–Roman historian and philosopher Arrian of Nicomedia put it, Alexander would have "never ceased campaigning, eventually competing with himself if no other rival had been left to surpass."[1]

In Europe, we have similar statements first from Napoleon, who regretted not being able to "expand into the universe" and later from British, French and German imperialists, for whom expansion eventually became everything and turned into an end in itself. As Hannah Arendt pointed out in *The Origins of Totalitarianism*, the staunch imperialists no longer aimed to achieve certain limited, strategic or economic ends but succumbed to the fascination of limitless expansion and boundless accumulation of power. One of the most notorious expressions of this boundless expansionary vision and urge came from Cecil Rhodes (1853–1902), the man responsible for

---

[1] As quoted in Robin Lane Fox, *Alexander the Great*, London 1973, 16.

Britain's augmentation in South Africa, whose dearest wish it was to transcend the limits of the globe and "annex the planets" if he could.[1]

At the same time, the transgression of national boundaries and the structural decline of the traditional bodies politic (i.e., the city or nation states) triggered a fundamental change of attitudes to politics, private life and war in the postclassical, post-national and post-expansionary ages of ancient Greece and modern Europe. While commitment to the polis or nation declined and the inclination to politics and military achievement decreased, people turned increasingly towards post-heroism, economic efficiency, private aspiration and care for the self. As we shall see further along, this extensive overthrow of attitudes and mentality not only provided for a striking disparity of values between the "old" worlds of postclassical Europe and Greece and the "new," ascending powers of America and Rome; it also made the Greeks and Europeans susceptible to subordination and prepared them to accept increased levels of political and military domination by the Romans and Americans respectively.

A third stage of historical development then saw the progressive emergence of a superpower gradually attributing to itself the role of a universal peacemaker and guarantor of international stability, prosperity and peace. In the case of antiquity, the once proud and mighty powers of Greece saw themselves eclipsed, reduced to second order status and finally turned into *provincias* by the vastly superior power of Rome (starting with the establishment of the province of Macedonia in 146 B.C. and formally ending with the provincialization of Ptolemaic Egypt in 31 B.C.). In a basically similar way, the nation states of Europe, which had once ruled wide sections of the politically and economically relevant world, have seen themselves outclassed by the new, hegemonic superpower of the United States. Once the center of the world, they have now become as secondary and subordinate in geopolitical and military respects in a new, U.S.-dominated world as the cities and municipalities of ancient Greece had once been in the age of Roman predominance and supremacy. Over long periods of time, however, the emergent superpowers (both of which being giants steeped in republican values and virtues, having acquired overwhelming levels of financial power, economic potential and military might)

[1] As quoted in Hannah Arendt, *The Origins of Totalitarianism*, New York 1951, 124.

confined themselves to a system of indirect hegemony and informal control, through which they granted protection, provided security and safeguarded freedom. Persistently reluctant to conquer and annex, they relied instead on a structure of alliances and bonds of mutual allegiance with the previously defeated powers of Greece and Europe respectively.

In a fourth and final stage of ancient history, Rome's republican institutions and informal hegemonic regime eventually proved unable to master the challenges of increased social inequality, mounting political polarization and overstretched hegemonial responsibility. As a consequence, they finally gave way to authoritarian domestic rule and imperial acquisition (immediate subjection) of the "old" Greek world first during the late stages of the Roman republic and later in the framework of a monarchical, "Caesarean" empire established since the late first century B.C.[1] Since the start of the second century B.C., the Roman republic gradually transformed itself from a benevolent patron and generous protector of Greek freedom into a master of subjugation and exploitation. Considering this study's basic analogical approach, however, this raises the central question as to whether there are any signs in current U.S. politics, society and culture indicating that the history of America may, at some point, take a similar turn and that America's republican institutions and informal hegemonic regime may, at some point, give way to tighter forms of control and classically imperial practices along the lines of what occurred in the late stages of the Roman republic. (In such a sense, Tomas Madden has speculated that the United States may, at some point, extend U.S. citizenship to its European allies and assume more comprehensive responsibility for Europe, as once was the case with the allies of ancient Rome;[2] in an even more radical proposal, the French philosopher Regis Debray has raised the prospect of Europe joining the United States in a single transAtlantic union and incorporating itself into America's imperial domain. Debray contemplates an expanded U.S.A. called "United

---

[1] At its largest extent, the empire eventually ruled over a quasi ubiquitous and world-encompassing civilization that reached from Spain to Syria and from Britain to North Africa.

[2] Thomas F. Madden, *Empires of Trust. How Rome built — and America is building — a New World*, New York 2008, 227. Madden's prospect has become a bit less improbable since the commencement of negotiations on a common free trade area between Europe and the United States — considering the numerous historical precedents of economic integration having paved the way for political coalescence, merger and integration.

States of the West" as the only way to protect the unity and values of the Occident against an imminent Islamic assault or Chinese dominance of the globe.[1])

Unlikely though it may seem today, there may come a time when republican America, like late republican Rome, will lack the capacity to cope with the burdens of mounting social polarization, increasing political tension and overstretched international responsibility — and hence resort to more repressive, authoritarian political practices at national and international level, structurally resembling those once embraced by late republican Rome. As we shall see and discuss in Chapter 13, seismic social, economic, political and military developments are underway indeed in present-day America, which bear a strong structural resemblance to the social, economic, political and military concussions once having undermined the stability, the foundations and the vigor of Rome's republican institutions in the late second and early first century B.C.

As for the final emergence of Caesarean, i.e., universal peace-preserving rule, however, which Spengler considered the ultimate stage of any high cultural entity or formation and of whose eventual ascendancy in the West he was therefore firmly convinced, it looks as though he himself did not always adhere consistently to his own analogical approach. Although referring repeatedly to the striking similarities between the ancient Romans and modern Americans — such as their political sobriety and pragmatic spirit, their pursuit of practical and technical success, or their preference for facts over metaphysical speculation — he does not persistently seem to have drawn the logical conclusions from his own theoretical and conceptual framework. For as the universal, Caesarean empire of the ancient world was only able to emerge in Rome and not in one of the city-states of ancient Greece, modern Caesarism cannot possibly arise in one of the European nation states but only in the United States itself, if the overall structural analogy is to be maintained. Provided it is true that Europe stands in the same relation to America as Greece had once stood to Rome, the prospective Caesar of the West can, by definition, only come to power in America.[2]

---

[1] Regis Debray, *Empire 2.0. A Modest Proposal for a United States of the West*, Berkeley 2004, 34s.

[2] Probably the most prominent commentator having warned explicitly of autocracy and "Caesarism" in America, as "the claims of omnipotence erode domestic restraints," has been Henry Kissinger (Henry Kissinger, *Does*

Spengler however seems to have believed that a modern, occidental Caesar could eventually prevail in Germany — viewing himself as a national political prophet, whose task it was to convince a young German elite of the need to embrace the inescapable fate of Western civilization and place itself at the service of a prospective German Caesar. Yet as ancient Greece had once surpassed the peak of its historical significance and vigor and was poised to be eclipsed by the new, emerging superpower of Rome, the Europe of the 1920s and 30s already faced the doom of submission and eclipse by a hugely mightier, more efficient and more energetic rival.

Taking seriously the conceptual analogy between the age of antiquity and the age of the West, the logical conclusion ought to have been that the great tasks of future international history — i.e., the global preservation of order, prosperity and peace — were no longer to be accomplished by the Europeans but by the United States. As Rome's task had once been to ensure the *pax Romana*, it was now to become America's mission to provide the *pax Americana*. (Quite logically, the dictatorial regime that came to power in Germany after 1933 bore resemblance not to the universal, peace-preserving empire of ancient Rome but rather — if any at all — to one of the ruthless tyrannies of late ancient Greece. Spengler himself soon realized that

---

America Need a Foreign Policy. Toward a New Diplomacy for the 21st Century, New York 2001, 287). — On the other hand, explicit analogies between Julius Caesar and George W. Bush have proved to be somewhat precipitate, as Bush's tenure has expired without the liquidation of American democracy, the cancellation of elections and the establishment of one-man rule, backed by regular U.S. troops or Blackwater Inc. — As for the critics having accused George W. Bush of ruling like a Caesar cf. Margaret Malamud, *Ancient Rome and Modern America*, Oxford 2008, 259s; Maria Wyke, "A Twenty-First Century Caesar," in: Maria Wyke (ed.), *Julius Caesar in Western Culture*, Malden/Mass. 2006, 305-323. After the invasion of Iraq, the journalist Brad Warthen wrote in affirmation of the president's single-mindedness and responsibility to act: "George W. Bush has crossed his Rubicon, and he has taken us with him. Julius Caesar set world history on a new course when he took his legion into Italy in defiance of the Senate. President Bush has taken an equally irrevocable step by entering the Tigris and Euphrates basin to wage war in spite of UN objection" (as quoted in Wyke, 318). In May 2003, Denise Giardina commented in the *Charleston Gazette* that Bush had "assumed the mantle of Julius Caesar. He is in the process of ruining the American republic and establishing an American / corporate empire" (as quoted in Wyke, 319). Still in 2006, Chalmers Johnson claimed that "Bush has unleashed a political crisis comparable to the one Julius Caesar posed for the Roman constitution. If the United States has neither the means nor the will to overcome this crisis, then we have entered the last days of the republic." (Chalmers Johnson, *Nemesis, The Last Days of the American Republic*, New York 2006, 244).

---

the Nazi movement was not the authoritarian Caesarean system he had striven for and envisaged. He found the Nazis vulgar, ideologically insane and too narrowly German, and he declined to make any further public appearance despite attempts by the Nazis to exploit his political and intellectual reputation.)

At the same time, the basic structural analogy between modern America and ancient Rome is scarcely sufficient reason to assume that American world supremacy might already be in its final stages and that new ascending powers like China or India might soon take over America's dominant role in world affairs. In fact, the power of America is still young and vigorous, and American predominance, as the supposedly ultimate stage of Western civilization, is still at a relatively early point of its life cycle[1] (given, in particular, that the U.S.A. still seems a sizeable distance away from reaching the point in the history of the high cultures and superpowers where liberty, republican government and informal, alliance-based hegemony are finally replaced with imperial, universal rule.) As a general fact, the (predominantly European) analysts and commentators predicting America's supposedly unstoppable decline or claiming that the end of American world supremacy may be virtually imminent tend to hugely underestimate the potency and power of America, and the vast economic, financial, military and diplomatic resources which the United States is able to mobilize around the world to assert itself in international politics and withstand any challenge to its dominant role on the global political stage. (To give a typical example, the French sociologist Emmanuel Todd has claimed that America's domestic decay and economic out performance by nations like India and China will make it impossible for the United States, in the medium term, to maintain its dominance in world affairs, providing Europe with the opportunity to emancipate itself from U.S. hegemony through closer collaboration with Russia. Since the United States could no longer afford its vast array of military liabilities in view of its enormous trade and budget deficits, it would have to resign itself, sooner rather than later, to the transition from a unipolar to a multipolar world.[2])

---

[1] This fact is also emphasized by Madden, 297.
[2] Cf. Emmanuel Todd, *After the Empire. The Breakdown of the American Order*, New York 2003. Other heralds of American decline included Paul Kennedy who predicted back in the 1980s that America would have to withdraw from positions abroad, reduce its expenditure on defense and share the burden of leadership with others, and that the pax Americana would soon become

In a structurally similar manner, many Hellenistic Greeks tended to believe, for long periods of time, that they could still afford challenging the superiority of Rome, only to find their armies defeated by the Roman legions and their leaders humiliated by the Roman generals and envoys time and time again — from the crushing defeat suffered by the Macedonian and Seleucid kings in the early second century B.C. down to the participation of many Greek city-states in the anti-Roman Mithridatic Wars, fought between 88 and 63 B.C., in the course of which Mithridates and his Greek allies were defeated by Sulla and finally removed from power by Pompey the Great. In modern history, the Germans in World War II and the Soviets in the Cold War era finally learned the hard way (and had to resign themselves to the fact) that there would not be a European nation again with the resources and capacity to defy the American superpower. In fact, world-embracing hegemonic powers like ancient Rome or modern America do not tend to abandon or lose their global predominance after only a few decades of sustained superpower status. Taking into account that Rome's overall trajectory and historical lifespan lasted more than 1,000 years and that, even after the downfall of the republic and the establishment of the empire in the first century B.C., the age of Roman world supremacy was still to continue for another five hundred years, all the indications are that, rather than having reached its final stages, the age of American world supremacy may only be in its infancy.[1]

On the other hand, it has become increasingly popular in recent years, in view of America's sole superpower status after the implosion of the USSR, its overwhelming superiority in military, technological and economic respects, its responsibility to maintain global peace and trade, its giant reach in terms of language, culture, lifestyles and ideas, and its vast network of allies, vassal nations and military bases around the world, to classify the United States as an *empire* — be it a *benevolent empire*, an empire driven by security interests and defensive motivations, an *empire by invitation*, a *liberal empire*, an *empire by denial*,

---

unsustainable due to military overstretch and the exhaustion of economic and financial resources. (Paul Kennedy, *The Rise and Fall of the Great Powers. Economic Change and Military Conflict from 1500 to 2000*, New York 1987)

[1] Robert Kagan may well have a point in claiming that "it is reasonable to assume that we have only just entered into a long era of American hegemony." (Robert Kagan, *Of Paradise and Power. America and Europe in the New World Order*, New York 2003, 88)

an *empire lite* or a *neo-conservative empire* with the universal mission of expanding democracy and capitalist, pro-market values, so as to bring salvation to the world and redemption from evil through military force.[1]

Yet whatever the nature of present-day USA may be, it is most certainly not an *empire proper* by Roman standards, comparable to the seven universal empires identified and analyzed by Spengler, all of which were engaged in policies of territorial acquisition, immediate subjection of other nations and direct governmental rule (or control) over the entirety of what they believed was the civilized world. Quite outspokenly, the conservative historian Daniel Kagan pointed out in 2006 that "all comparisons between America's current place in the world and anything legitimately called an empire in the past reveal ignorance and confusion about any reasonable meaning of the concept of empire, especially the Roman empire.... The Romans acquired the greatest part of their empire by direct military conquest, subjected their people to Roman law, and imposed taxes and compulsory military service under Roman command... To compare the United States with any such empire is ludicrous."[2]

At the end of the day, the standard of reference and comparison for present-day America is not the Roman Empire, but still the Roman republic and its informal hegemonic regime. In ancient history, it took the Romans roughly 150 years to proceed from the rise to unrivaled superpower status after the victorious Second Punic War in 201 B.C. and the defeat of the Hellenistic powers, i.e., Macedonia and Syria in 197 and 190 B.C., to the factual liquidation of the republic when Caesar told his troops to cross the Rubicon in 49 B.C. Bearing

---

[1]   Eric Adler, "Post 9/11 Views of Rome and the Nature of 'Defensive Imperialism'," in: *International Journal of the Classical Tradition* 15 (2008), 587-610; G. John Ikenberry, "American Power and the Empire of Capitalist Democracy," in: Michael Cox et al. (eds.), *Empires, Systems and States. Great Transformations in International Politics*, Cambridge 2001, 191-212; Richard H. Immermann, *Empire for Liberty. A History of American Imperialism from Benjamin Franklin to Paul Wolfowitz*, Princeton/New York/Oxford 2010; Michael Cox, "Empire? The Bush Doctrine and the Lessons of History," in: David Held / Mathias Koenig-Archibuge (eds.), *American Power in the Twenty-First Century*, Malden/Mass. 2004, 21-51; Michael Ignatieff, *Empire Lite, Nation-Building in Bosnia, Kosovo and Afghanistan*, Toronto 2003. By Empire Lite, Ignatieff understands a hegemonic power ready to stage military interventions and temporarily occupy other countries in order to enforce democracy, free markets and human rights, backed by the most awesome military power of all time.
[2]   As quoted in Wyke, 312.

this in mind, it seems unlikely for the United States to undergo the same process in only 25 years after its rise to lone superpower status following victory in the Cold War and the implosion of the USSR in 1991. As Niall Ferguson has rightly claimed, America's "republican constitution has withstood the ambitions of any would be Caesars — so far. It is of course early days. The United States is 228 years old. When Caesar crossed the Rubicon, the Roman Republic was 460 years old."[1]

At the end of the day it remains to be seen what the future has in store for America and whether the United States is indeed so exceptional and different from everything else having existed so far in the history of the world that it will not follow the trajectory described by Spengler and stand as the one lone exception to the rule of great universal powers abandoning liberty and turning imperial.[2]

In fact, it may well be argued — considering the many similarities recognizable between the challenges and seismic changes facing the Roman republic after its rise to sole superpower status in 190 B.C. and the challenges and seismic changes facing America after the fall of the USSR — that the USA is already about to enter into the early stages of a pre-imperial culture and power-political condition. Taking into account that the rise of Rome to lone superpower status in the early second century B.C. also marked the beginning of its late republican, pre-imperial period, there is reason to reflect on whether the United States, at the outset of the 21st century, may have reached a similar point in its history.

Is the point of reference and standard of comparison for present-day America to be found in late republican Rome, and is the United States heading toward the same fate endured by the increasingly crisis-stricken Roman republic in the first century B.C.? The mere fact that, in its current stage of history, the United States does not correspond to the age of Caesar, the emperors and the praetorian guards (i.e., is not an empire proper), does not necessarily mean it

---

[1] Niall Ferguson, *Colossus. The Rise and Fall of the American Empire*, London 2004, 34.

[2] In this respect, it sounds precipitate to hold, as Peter Bender has done, that ancient Rome and modern America differ greatly in terms of "the final result, as a monarchically governed imperium on the one hand contrasts with a democratically and economically managed informal empire on the other." (Peter Bender, *Weltmacht Amerika. Das neue Rom*, Munich 2005, 23.) At the end of the day, however, the history of America is not yet over, and it still remains to be seen what the "final result" of U.S. history will be.

will never do so — i.e., develop into a global, universal empire ruled by autocratic means, fulfilling the task of ensuring free global commerce and trade and protecting the entirety of civilized mankind by means of its military might. After all, these are in fact early days in U.S. history, and it was by no means accidental that Oswald Spengler did not expect Caesarean rule (or Caesarism) to firmly establish itself in the West, in a fully developed form, before the year 2100.

To fully comprehend the concurrences and parallels of modern America and ancient Rome, however, and to address the question of whether political and socio-cultural developments are in place in present-day America that bear resemblance to basic political occurrences and socio-cultural trends of late republican Rome, we must first take a closer look at the postclassical ages of Greece and Europe respectively. For during the ages of Hellenistic Greece and post-imperialist Europe, seismic structural changes and shifts of attitude and mentality occurred, which gave rise to a striking disparity of values between the "old" worlds of Europe and Greece and the "new," ascending powers of America and Rome. As we shall see, a thorough analysis of this disparity of values will prove indispensable not only for understanding the Greek and European context itself but also for comprehending the basic characteristics of Roman and American power, political culture and mental constitution.

3. HELLENISTIC CULTURE, PHILOSOPHY AND ART — APOLITICISM, PRIVATE ASPIRATION AND SELF-REALIZATION[1]

The first of the great transitions to be reviewed in the framework of this essay will be the transition from classical to postclassical Greece and classical to postclassical (or post-imperialist) Europe. As for ancient Greece, the mental constitution and political culture in the age of Hellenism, i.e., the period after the death of Alexander the Great in 323 B.C. and the disintegration of his empire into the kingdoms of the *diadochi*, vastly differed from those of the classical age — considered by Spengler as the inescapable consequence of bio-societal ageing and natural exhaustion, as a tiring civilization becomes unable to preserve the attained levels of cultural fertility and political vigor.

In the Hellenistic period, the citizens developed increasingly reluctant attitudes to politics and war and the pursuit of political or military fame. Participation in the political arena, which had once been the splendor of life and embodiment of freedom for the citizens of Athens and the other city-states, now came to be regarded not as an honor but as a burden and an unreasonable constraint, preventing people from pursuing their own private ends. The fascination of politics and the willingness of citizens to actively participate in the city's political life — which had once given

---

[1] General works and collections on the Hellenistic period include: Glenn R. Bugh (ed.), *The Cambridge Companion to the Hellenistic World*, Cambridge/Mass. 2006; R. Malcolm Errington, *A History of the Hellenistic World, 323 — 30 B.C.*, Malden/Mass. 2008; Frank William Walbank, *The Hellenistic World* (German edition), Munich 1983.

rise to Aristotle's definition of the human being as a "zoon politicon" — declined dramatically. Athenians, for instance, grew increasingly weary of political activity, ultimately demanding financial incentives in return for attending the popular assemblies. To keep the democratic system going, the first 1,000 participants of a popular assembly were eligible to receive an attendance gratification of 3 *oboles* from the late fourth century B.C. onwards.

Moreover, orators like Isocrates and politicians like Eubulus advised their fellow citizens to abstain from political ambition and military undertakings, as only peace and moderation could spare them the oppressive cost of armament and secure the standard of living, whereas war and political ambition had only brought misery and distress. With a new generation of upper class youths anxious to avoid military service, the city-states grew increasingly irrelevant in military and geopolitical terms. In Athens, the number of young men attending the Ephebos, i.e., the city's traditional military training institution, dropped from 600 in 330 B.C. to an almost ridiculous 29 in 250 B.C. At the same time, the Greek *poleis* of the fourth and third century B.C. drastically reduced their levels of expenditure on defense, eager to use the saved financial resources for the sake of economic prosperity and wealth.

While life had once revolved around serving the institutions of the city-state, and citizens of the classical period had taken pride in actively shaping their municipal affairs, many postclassical Greeks now tried to evade the political and military duties and sought dispensation from the obligation to hold public office (such as the functions of judge and civil servant, the responsibility for grain and food supply, construction, public finances, defense, the restoration of temples, statues and gymnasiums, donations of oil and the organization of municipal cults and games). Increasingly, such functions were performed by private sponsors, rich individuals from a limited number of upper-class families or one of the Hellenistic monarchs as a public benefactor (*eurgetes*) rather than by the citizenry as a whole.

Whereas the influence of councils and popular assemblies declined and the former passion of politics and public discourse gave way to moderation and indifference, the communities became essentially dependent on the receipt of donations from rich benefactors, and municipal finance and administration were no longer governed by democratic decision-making but by the grace of wealthy families and individuals. Some of the eurgetes or public benefactors — such as the Macedonian king Cassander — were even held in divine veneration by a citizenry that had once so firmly insisted on its autonomy and vigorously refused to tolerate any master over its political (or municipal) affairs.

At the same time, we can observe concurrent developments in the intellectual and philosophical sphere. Ascending and rising to prominence in the postclassical age, Stoic philosophy conceived the universe as being essentially governed by god's unalterable will, so that the course of events is pre-determined by divine force and man can only resign himself to what happens and affirm his own unchangeable fate. The axiomatically deterministic convictions of Stoicism — where man's only freedom is the inner freedom of accepting basically unalterable outside processes, governed by an omnipresent divine logos to which the individual is helplessly exposed[1] — is a symptom of how much the former confidence of citizens in their power to shape the world by political means (i.e., by acting in concert with one's fellow-citizens) had decreased. The Stoic view that man can exercise control only over his inner mental affairs, consciousness and states of mind but not over outside circumstances (like poverty or wealth, power or suppression, honor or death) — which he must therefore disregard as not affecting his true human essence — shows the extent to which postclassical Greeks had lost their trust in the capacity to shape the outside world and govern their own destinies and lives through joint, collective political action. Instead of acting in concert with their fellow-citizens, postclassical Greeks tended to believe that man can only make a minimal impact on the state of the outside world and is hence required to occupy himself primarily with controlling his inner perceptions, seek quietude as a recipe for happiness (the apatheia of the Stoics and the ataraxia of the Epicureans) and focus on the examination of conscience, individual introspection and constant self-perfection of the soul.[2]

---

[1] Cf. A.A. Long, *From Epicurus to Epictetus. Studies in Hellenistic and Roman Philosophy*, Oxford/New York 2006, 152.

[2] Cf. Long, *From Epicurus to Epictetus*, 181. The disinclination to political activity was of course shared as well by the rising force of skepticism, which regarded all matters of the world as vain and not worthy of occupation by enlightened human beings.

As the desire to attain honor and fame in politics and war declined, the focus shifted increasingly towards economic prosperity and the care for private individual needs. In the third and partially the second century B.C., i.e., in the early years of Roman dominance and patronage, the Greek world prospered economically, as living standards rose, property and grain speculation flourished, international trade expanded, shipping companies prospered and the quantity and quality of goods increased.[1] Generally, the Hellenistic world developed a new, more efficient and systematic approach to the economy, which came to be based increasingly on financial and banking transactions, international maritime trade, factories, mines and the large-scale utilization of free and slave labor. At the same time, a culture of pleasure, entertainment, leisure and amusement arose especially in the large, cosmopolitan *megacities* like Alexandria, Antiochia or Seleukia, and elegance, luxury and wealth were displayed in a manner unthinkable in the morally rigorous and strait-laced classical age. While the role and power of the popular assemblies decreased, privately sponsored festivals, games, processions and sporting contests increased enormously in the Hellenistic period. Compared to the war-shaken times of the classical age, much of the Hellenistic period was marked by relative prosperity, pleasance and peace. In general, this was no longer an age of politics and politicians but rather of technological and scientific experts aiming to find new, efficient methods of exploiting raw materials and human ability, as major sections of the old elite withdrew from politics in favor of banking, finance and trade. In turn, the obligation to serve the state and hold public office came to be regarded as a burden and undue interference into the private aspirations of the individual, i.e., the pursuit of personal happiness, wealth and peace of mind. Whereas political activity was increasingly considered ignoble, the education, development and continuous examination of the human soul came to be perceived as the true essence and higher purpose in life.

The Hellenistic philosophies, notably the teachings of Epicurus, explicitly abandoned the quest for political fame and argued for a comprehensive withdrawal from public to private life, as they recommended people to seek apolitical happiness in explicit seclusion from the city and its institutions. Epicurus himself insisted on being

---

[1] Claude Mossé, *Athens in Decline 404–86 B.C.* (German edition), Munich/ Zurich 1979, 205.

a strictly private person who strove to abstain from politics, live in seclusion and concentrate entirely on his mental balance, physical wellbeing and peace of mind. Rather than politics and civic action, postclassical philosophy attended to emotions, individual happiness, physical wellbeing, comfort of the soul, and the inner struggles of the self. Basically, the new philosophies no longer searched for the ideal political constitution but tried to provide guidance for everyday individual behavior, concentrating in the first instance on practical ethics and essentially personal, subjective worries, needs and concerns.[1]

The general trend to apoliticism was not only reflected however in the area of philosophy but in virtually all segments of Hellenistic culture, including literature, drama and art: whereas the old, classical theater epitomized by Aristophanes had occupied itself primarily with the city's political life and municipal affairs, the new comedy — most prominently represented by Menander — ridiculed political ambition and the desire for greatness, concentrating instead on the small virtues and vices, the sweetness of private life and the pursuit of money, luxury and love. Whereas the old comedy had concerned itself with the political and social situation of Athens, the new Hellenistic comedy presented episodes from private everyday life, individual states of mind, marital intrigues and love affairs.[2]

As a general fact, life became less strict and more permissive in the Hellenistic age. The poems of Theocritus frankly dealt with vulgar and sexual topics, and love relationships and eroticism came to dominate the world of literature, theater and art. At the same time, sculpture no longer presented the exemplary young, heroic and self-disciplined citizen-soldier but rather members of the lower class like beggars, farmers or fishermen, who overtly displayed states of emotion, passion and pain. While a strict distinction had been in place between public and private life, and emotions were not supposed to be shown in public in the classical age, individuals were now encouraged to indulge in personal states of emotion and give vent to personal feelings.

---

[1] The basic detachment of Hellenistic philosophy from politics is also acknowledged by A. A. Long, From Epicurus to Epictetus, 21.
[2] For a comprehensive discussion of Hellenistic theater and art cf. G. Shipley, *The Greek World after Alexander, 323–30 BC*, London 2000, 256ss.

The rise of non-heroic values and the degradation of politics and war, i.e., the areas of society previously reserved for men, also came along with a general reassessment of the social role of women.[1] In particular, Stoic and Epicurean philosophy endorsed the equal treatment of women, who were explicitly encouraged to participate in the philosophical circles of the postclassical age (in fact, Epicurus is said to have once called himself a man in women's clothing, figuratively speaking, to remind his followers of the need to take one's bearings more extensively from female virtues, values and behaviors).

During the Hellenistic age, women increasingly appeared in public and abandoned their traditional confinement to the household or *oikos*. Moreover, women also came to play an ever-greater role in Hellenistic (post heroic) literature, drama and art. Wealthy upper-class women were held in high public esteem as donors, heads of religious associations, benefactors and priests, as the steadily spreading and advancing mystery cults no longer distinguished between females and males. Female poets received public honors, and women attained the right to conclude contracts, acquire landed properties and perform financial transactions. Especially among the upper classes, marriage was progressively considered a relationship in which the mutual love and respect of both sexes was to replace the older notion of unquestioned male predominance. From the second century B.C. onwards, divorce became a fairly straightforward business, easy to bring about by either the husband or the wife. Following completion of the divorce, the dowry was no longer retained by the husband but was returned to the family of the wife.

In addition, art no longer presented the woman merely as a housewife and mother but in progressively permissive ways. Interest in the female physiognomy increased in the area of medicine, and the "bathing woman" became an established motif and feature of advanced Hellenistic art. In Asia Minor, the famous Aphrodite of Knidos as the first Greek depiction of a nude female body soon turned into a tourist attraction for viewers from across the Hellenistic world.

In general, the extensive reassessment of the woman's role within society and culture reflects a post heroic turn, fundamentally

---

[1] The new social and cultural role of the woman is discussed by R. van Bremen, "Woman and Wealth," in: A. Cameron/A. Kuhrt (eds.), *Images of Women in Antiquity*, London 1993, 223-242; Dorothy J. Thompson, "The Hellenistic Family," in: Bugh (ed.), 93-112.

distinguishing the Hellenistic period from the classical age as a time of male predominance where the crucial areas of politics and civil defense were strictly reserved for men, and women (especially among the social and political elites) had been confined to public invisibility and seclusion in the oikos or house.

4. The Degradation of the Polis

Yet how can this wholesale change of attitudes, the depreciation of political activity and ambition, and the appreciation of private aspiration and personal interest, be explained? Is Hellenism's turn towards new, post heroic values only — as Spengler claimed — a consequence of bio-societal ageing, attributable to a loss of vigor and the transition from a young and fertile *culture* to a tired and exhausted *civilization*? Or is it possible, after all, to find essentially analytic, rational and causal explanations for this comprehensive change of attitudes to life and fundamental re-definition of values?

Obviously, the key development of post-classical Greek history was a general decline of the city-state and municipal body politic, around which classical Greek politics and culture had once been centered. In fact, already the famous orator Isocrates of Athens understood that, after the endeavors and devastations of the Peloponnesian War, the historical role of the city-state was played out and the Greeks could only hope to exert any relevant influence on the future course of international history and affairs by rallying behind Philip of Macedonia. In 338 B.C., at the latest, after suffering devastating defeat at the battle of Chaeronea, the city-states saw themselves eclipsed, reduced to second order status and forced into semi-dependence by Macedonia. By that time, it had become evident that the powers to fulfill the great tasks of future international history would no longer be the municipalities and city-states of mainland Greece. With the rise of Alexander the Great and the subsequent establishment of the large Hellenistic kingdoms, the city-states and their citizens saw themselves exposed to powers too large for them to handle.

Yet in the same measure as the city-states ceased being the makers of history and citizens ceased believing that their traditional bodies politic — exhausted by the endeavors and devastations of decades of war — could ever regain their former greatness and grandeur, the incentive to engrave one's name in the immortal chronicles of the city began losing its (formerly overwhelming) appeal. While the democratic institutions of the city-states remained basically and extrinsically intact in the Hellenistic age and even in the time of Roman predominance until the establishment of the empire in the first century B.C., the active participation of citizens, and the passion which city politics had once evoked, progressively wore away. As city politics began to lack the great agenda that once unleashed the energies and ambitions of public life, it was only logical that the citizens' desire for honor and fame through individual distinction in politics and war decreased. As the major policymakers were no longer the city politicians but the monarchs of the large Hellenistic kingdoms, the once great incentive to gain immortal fame as a furtherer, servant and defender of the polis lost much of its attraction and appeal.

It is against this backdrop that the decline of the municipal spirit and the rise of apolitical attitudes, especially among the former political elites, must be assessed: as the once all-embracing relationship between the city and the citizen faltered and the polis was no longer experienced as a protecting association absorbing civic energies and endeavors, the result was increased personal emancipation, individualization and room for the pleasures and aspirations of private life. Instead of placing oneself at the service of the state and becoming engaged in politics and public life, the citizens now focused on the benefits of peace, economic prosperity, scientific achievement, personal concerns and subjective states of mind.[1] With the polis no longer considered the focus of life absorbing civic energies and aspirations, the citizens now experienced themselves primarily as individuals, occupied with matters of private life and essentially personal, physical and mental concerns. Intellectually, this trend is reflected in the fact that virtually all Hellenistic philosophy was basically individualistic and politically indifferent. Stoicism,

---

[1] For the Hellenistic period as an age of science, commerce and trade, see also Chapter 5.

Epicureanism and Cynicism no longer concerned themselves substantially with political and social issues or searching for the ideal form of government and political constitution. Instead of discussing collective political action and civic organization, they concentrated on the examination of individual conscience, the search for personal happiness, the observation of inwardness and the needs and inner struggles of the self.

Hellenistic philosophy busied itself no longer with devising a general political and moral order conducive to the institutions of the city-state but with self-scrutiny and self-improvement, sustained balance of mind and the practical ethical behavior of the individual without respect of political frameworks, conditions and forms.[1] As the pleasures of political responsibility, civic action and self-administration faltered, the readiness to assume political responsibility decreased and many Greeks left the (protective) narrowness of their traditional poleis to become subjects of the large Hellenistic kingdoms, a general inclination resulted to withdraw from politics, concentrate on self-sufficiency and focus one's mind on essentially personal worries, individual needs and subjective concerns.

Finally, the trend was very much the same as well in terms of religious practice: Whereas the function of religion in the classical age had been to uphold the power and authority of the city-state and provide collective identity for members of the polis, wide sections of society in the Hellenistic age embraced the mysteries of Isis and Osiris, Cybele or Serapis, which aimed for individual salvation, personal guidance and mental equilibrium rather than for the common good and prosperity of the polis.[2] While the old, municipal gods of classical religion had been tied inseparably to particular temples, places and institutions of the city, the mystery cults transgressed such limits and reached out beyond the confines of the polis, thus reflecting the generally diminished levels of loyalty and devotion to the political and institutional framework of the city-state.

---

[1] Cf. Shipley, 64s.
[2] Jon D. Mikalson, "Greek Religion. Continuity and Change in the Hellenistic Period," in: Bugh (ed.), 208-222, 211; Walbank, 211ss.

5. European Mentalities of the Post-Imperialist Age

The age of European expansion and imperial supremacy extended at the latest to 1945, when the French and British empires were poised for liquidation, Nazi Germany's attempt to establish a "German India" in the east of Europe through a war of colonization had failed, and the nations of Europe had abandoned their former claim to be the major actors of international politics and history. In this "postclassical" Europe, like in Hellenistic Greece, the political and intellectual atmosphere has been marked by a massive decline of heroism and patriotic sentiment and a turn towards explicitly non-heroic values like prosperity, affluence, peace, personal enjoyment and individual self-realization. Like the postclassical Greeks, postwar Europeans have become reluctant to make personal sacrifices for the sake of their nations or bodies politic that might distract them from pursuing their own private ends.

Essentially, Europe's postwar era is an age no longer of politics and political ambition but of economic and scientific efficiency, as the passion of politics has decreased extensively in comparison to the pre-war period. In ancient history, Athens grew irrelevant in military and geopolitical terms, but it was a pleasant place to live, especially in the third century B.C. Similarly, living standards in Europe have risen to unprecedented levels after the end of Europe's imperialist age and expansionist career — in an age dominated by technology, applied science, consumerism, mass communication, motorization and entertainment.[1] Generally, postwar Europeans are anxious to avoid ambitious geopolitical ventures, which are widely considered a disturbing element threatening the pursuit of prosperity, comfort, tranquility and peace. No longer comprehending the readiness of citizens in the classical age to fight and for idealist causes, for one's own language, one's own culture or "for a piece of land"[2], they consider themselves more enlightened and morally advanced than their allegedly narrow-minded ancestors and predecessors. In fact, the objective of the Europeans is no longer to make history but to evade history, as they relish mediocrity and lack the will (or find it inappropriate) to sacrifice their own personal interests for the benefit and splendor of the nation. Rather than harboring large-scale political aspirations, they focus on "what must never happen again," keen to contain the repercussions of history and prevent the re-emergence of national ambition, as they indulge in a culture of memory and prefer seeing themselves as the victims rather than the actors of history (including the erection of statues to victims rather than to heroes or combatants for their country. Indeed, Europe's present-day culture of memory and recollection bears a structural resemblance to the Hellenistic age, which was a time not so much of one's own poetic, literary and artistic creation but rather of collecting, editing and scientifically analyzing the great works and cultural achievements of the classical age.[3])

At the end of the day, these trends reflect a general abandonment of the wish to actively shape the world by political means and resignation to the fact that the days of great historical achievement, cultural

---

[1] In fact, Hellenistic Greece in the third century B.C. (which thus in many ways resembles late 19th and early 20th century Europe) was the heyday of science with the creation of colossal libraries, research and teaching centers and remarkable achievements in mathematics, mechanical engineering, astronomy, botany, zoology and medicine, but also in technological and military terms with its gigantic lighthouses, warships, catapults and siege towers/machines. This period was followed by an age dominated by capitalists, merchants, bankers, commercial shipping companies, metropolises, imperial trading routes and free urban labor in the internationalized economy of late Hellenistic Greece and by the age of economic prosperity, consumerism, higher living standards, motorization, commodities production, mass communication and mass media consumption that began constituting Europe since the end of World War I and, in particular, since 1945.

[2] Cf. Spengler, 661.

[3] The same applies to the playful transfer of classical cultural elements into new contexts, which has been a characteristic feature both of the Hellenistic period and of post-war Europe (for the Hellenistic context, cf. Krevens/Sens, 195).

creation and political struggle are over. Just as postclassical Greeks praised the benefits of peace and sought to reduce expenditure on the armed forces to use the saved financial resources for economic ends, postwar Europeans tend to hold pacifist views, focus on economic prosperity and concentrate on the pleasures of private life, readily embracing a culture of softness and effeminacy. Eager to reduce their spending on defense, they find themselves admonished by the United States to upgrade their armies and spend minimum shares of GDP on defense, so as to retain the capacity of making relevant contributions to the preservation of international stability, order and peace. In the Hellenistic age, the city-states of ancient Greece drastically reduced their armed forces, and the Roman historian Livy accused the Athenians of "only having fought with words" in the First Macedonian War. In a similar manner, postwar Europeans are anxious to limit themselves to diplomacy and abstain from the use of military force — causing the American publicist Max Boot to mock that "the only thing the French army is good for is teaching other armies how to surrender properly."[1] In fact, the military irrelevance of postwar Europe structurally resembles the situation of postclassical Greece in the time of Roman predominance and supremacy, when Athens, Sparta, Pergamum and Rhodes had smaller armies than ever before and came to rely entirely on the protection and patronage by a superpower, which treated them, at least initially, in conspicuously benevolent ways. One of the most striking manifestations of Roman disdain for the political and military impotence of Greece (or, in other words: of the circumstance that the Romans no longer took the Greeks seriously as a political and military factor) was that, from the first century B.C. onwards, upper-class Romans began viewing and visiting the cities of Greece as parts of a large historical and military museum — like present-day American tourists who experience the cities and landscapes of Europe as a large-scale cultural museum or destination theme park holding the treasures of the Western past.[2] In both cases, the sites and countries perceived and visited as museums are places where people no longer wish to expose themselves to the risks and threats facing those who are still willing to be genuine makers of history and forceful actors of international politics.

---

[1] Max Boot, "Plädoyer für ein Empire," in: Ulrich Speck/ Natan Sznaider (eds.), *Empire Amerika. Perspektiven einer neuen Weltordnung*, Munich 2003, 60-70.
[2] Cf. Madden, 114.

At the same time, the underlying situation is likewise very similar insofar as postwar Europeans, like the Hellenistic Greeks, are firmly convinced that their traditional bodies politic, i.e., the nation states, are no longer capable of meeting the requirements of a new age. In fact, already during the late nineteenth century and in the age of high imperialism, the dynamics of industrial production and capitalist accumulation challenged the boundaries of the nation state, whose institutions and markets were increasingly regarded as being too small and hence as posing obstacles to the dynamic unfolding of productive market forces. All the more after 1945, Europeans tended to be convinced that their traditional framework of nation states — exhausted and devastated after two world wars and shocked by the experience of defeat and military inferiority, which almost all the nations of Europe suffered in 1939/1945 — was no longer capable of being a match for the vastly superior potential, economic might and military machine of the United States, which was to establish itself successfully as the new epicenter of international politics.

As Paul Kennedy showed in *The Rise and Fall of the Great Powers*, the United States overtook the nations of Europe in terms of manufacturing output already in the early 20th century and dwarfed the European powers in GDP and war potential during and after World War II.[1] After the war, the Europeans quickly resigned themselves to the newly arisen power structure, eagerly shifting the responsibility for international politics to the United States and seeking shelter under America's protective shield. Having lost their former confidence and belief in the capability of their traditional, national bodies politic, the postwar Europeans — like the Hellenistic Greeks in ancient history — no longer sense the ambition to make history; instead, they believe their best option is to keep out of risky international affairs as far as possible and wait for the United States to assume responsibility and leadership.

As European politics lacks the great agenda of the past, and confidence in the nation state has faltered, it is only logical that people in postwar Europe increasingly turn their backs on politics, focusing instead on private aspiration, introspection, personal pleasure and self-realization. By and large, the prevailing attitude among present-

---

[1]   Kennedy, 332ss., 354-369. According to Kennedy's figures, the United States accounted for 50% of global industrial output, 57% of global steel production and 75% of global passenger car production in 1947.

day European citizens is to shy away from international political responsibility, disregard notions of national glory and live essentially private lives of prosperity, tranquility and peace.[1] With great political struggle and ambition considered to be a thing of the past, political debates and intellectual ideas in postwar Europe lack the boldness, ferocity and passion of the classical age, as they tend to taste of moderation and *juste milieu* instead of the former national, religious or ideological zeal (so that present-day Europeans often feel bewildered at the heated political debates and vibrant political life in the United States).

By contrast to its classical period, postwar Europe is no longer the place of vigorous political struggle and lively intellectual debate which once captured the attention of the globe, as they were poised to determine the future course of international history and the destiny and fortune of the world. (Instead, this global attention is now captured by events and debates in the United States, and U.S. elections are the only ones that really matter, while the names of present-day European politicians are unlikely to achieve more than footnote status in future global history books.) With the center of global politics having shifted away from Europe to the United States, present-day internal affairs within the European nations have become largely non-relevant in global history terms except for occasions when the nations of Europe interact with America or when the U.S. forms coalitions with its European client (or vassal) nations. From a structural point of view, Europe after World War II hence resembles the situation of ancient Greece in the age of Roman dominance and supremacy, which considered its own history to be essentially over and whose inner affairs sank into insignificance in global history terms except for times, in which Rome interacted with the Greeks or Greece became the scene and subject of Roman activity and intervention.

Anxious to evade the repercussions of history, postwar Europeans seek to leave the preservation of global peace and the use of military force to the United States — thus bearing a strong resemblance to the Hellenistic Greeks, who expected the Romans to provide for their (military) protection and take charge of their international

---

[1] As Robert Kagan has stated, the Europeans have opted for a world of "transnational negotiations and international cooperation, a postheroic paradise of peace and relative prosperity" (Kagan, 7).

affairs, which they had once been so passionate about in the days of the classical age. In fact, the city-states of Hellenistic Greece gradually lost the capacity of coping with their own internal and external affairs in terms of foreign policy, administration and defense. Instead, they started appealing to Roman senators and generals, asking for protection, preferential treatment and resolution of their own internal matters including the settlement of border disputes, the confirmation of privileges and the administration of justice. Time and time again, they would send delegations to Rome, expecting benefaction from Roman politicians, senators and generals whom they requested to take care of their interests and act as arbitrators resolving the perpetual quarrels in and between the city-states.

Increasingly, the Hellenistic Greeks even felt offended that Rome, as a hegemon, did not properly meet its duty of care, failing to look after the affairs of Greece on a sustained basis and regularly withdrawing its troops after having brought an only shaky order and preliminary peace to the Hellenistic east. Often, we can hear them complaining that the Romans confined themselves to sending embassies and did not sufficiently meet their duties, which, from the Greeks' point of view, they were obliged to do as just and responsible rulers. (In a later stage though, especially since the first century B.C., Greek complaints no longer referred to a deficit of Roman attention but rather to the replacement of benevolent rule with excessive taxation and financial exploitation.) For long periods of time, the Greeks kept looking for a savior and patron center, on whom their hopes and desires could focus and who would finally arrange for their lasting security and order. Eventually, a benevolent patron of such kind seemed to have arisen in the person of Pompey the Great who, as an army commander, provided for a comprehensive reorganization of Greece through a system of client kingdoms, the permanent deployment of Roman troops, and effective ways of combating piracy in 67 B.C. For the first time, a figure had hence emerged who showed a genuine sense of responsibility for the Greek world, promised to guarantee long-term security and peace, and was therefore celebrated by the Greeks as a savior and benefactor fulfilling the ideal of a "good king" along Hellenistic images and lines.

Apart from that, the inclination among the Hellenistic Greeks to evade political responsibility became apparent not only in their semi-religious reverence for Pompey, Flaminius and other Roman leaders but also in the decision taken by the rulers of several Hellenistic kingdoms, i.e., Pergamum, Cyrene and Bithynia, to will their nations to the Senate of Rome in 129, 96 and 74 B.C. respectively. In fact, the Romans did not usurp responsibility for the cities and states of Hellenistic Greece but were urged to assume such responsibility due to the increasing inability of the cities and states to govern their own affairs. Whenever war broke out, the Hellenistic kingdoms collapsed like houses of cards in the face of a few Roman legions and, soon afterwards, showed an astonishing readiness and preparation to accept their transformation into protectorates under Roman patronage and rule.

Like the city-states of mainland Hellenistic Greece, which became dependent on Roman protection against the hegemonic aspirations of Macedonia (or Persia), postwar Europeans have sought protection against a possible Soviet assault from the superior political and military might of the United States, which they have entrusted with the enforcement of international security and the maintenance of international peace.

Just as postclassical Greeks were in need of Roman arbitration and intervention, postwar Europeans have become structurally unable to resolve their own internal disputes and external affairs. In virtually every international crisis and on virtually every international issue, the nations of Europe find themselves at odds, speaking with multiple voices and incapable of taking joint effective action, until finally they hear a call to order from America. This pattern became most obvious in the U.S. intervention into the civil wars that followed the collapse of Yugoslavia in 1991, for which the Europeans themselves proved unable to find a solution due to internal discord, military impotence and incapacity to act — but also in the inability of Europe to develop a common approach to America's "War on Terror" and the "Coalition of the Willing" after 9/11/2001. Even in one of Europe's innermost affairs, it took an intervention by U.S. president Obama and the physical presence of U.S. finance minister Timothy Geithner to prevent the Europeans from kicking Greece out of the eurozone and thus endangering the future of the single European currency system in 2012.

In summary, the geopolitical impotence of postclassical Greece and post-imperialist Europe traces back to a loss of commitment to the inherited bodies politic, a decline of confidence in one's own political frameworks and institutions. Firmly convinced that the historical role of the inherited, municipal or national bodies politic is played out, the Greeks and Europeans ceased believing in their capacity to make international history and assert themselves on the international political stage. Instead, they long for relief from the burden of history-making and international responsibility, which they expect to be assumed by Rome and the United States respectively.

Not least, this becomes reflected in the fact that American presidents like Kennedy or Obama have been revered as saviors and hailed as deliverers by the Europeans in a manner similar to how Pompey the Great, Flaminius and other Roman leaders were once revered as benefactors and praised as saviors by the cities and states of Hellenistic Greece.[1] Whereas Greeks and Europeans of the classical age had regarded their political systems, i.e., the polis and the nation state, as the epitomes of civilization and role models for the rest of the world, this original confidence and belief is no longer to be found among the Hellenistic Greeks and postwar Europeans. Today, only the Americans remain convinced that the rest of the world ought to emulate their political system, cultural practices and economic ways. By contrast, the Europeans are anxious to avoid relapsing into "Eurocentricsm," as they have lost the former desire to acquire and exercise power or impose their will on others. Embracing the idea that the nations of Europe have no further historical mission to fulfill, they are eager to opt out of global politics and readily resign themselves to a progressive decline in weight on the international political stage.

No longer believing that they still have historical missions to fulfill and considering their historical energies to be used up, many Europeans no longer see a need to preserve the qualities that it takes to assert oneself in the global political arena. While the Americans establish think tanks for a "New American Century" and consider their nation a "city on the hill," to which all others look in hope, many Europeans believe that by the end of the 21st century their nations may no longer exist, and narratives of ascension (or aspirations of national greatness) have long been replaced with fears of decline.

---

[1] For the latter cf. Betty Forte, *Rome and the Romans how the Greeks Saw Them*, Rome 1972, 134.

Subscribing to the notion that the nations of Europe no longer have the power and capacity to shape the world by political means, postwar Europeans have lost their passion for politics, turned their focus to personal aspiration, and aim to live essentially private, post-heroic lives of tranquility, self-realization, prosperity and comfort (while the levels of indifference about public affairs are steadily on the rise and patriotic conviction continuously declines).

In doing so, however, they bear striking resemblance indeed to the Hellenistic Greeks (especially Stoic and Epicurean philosophy), for whom it likewise became a guiding principle to withdraw from politics and occupy oneself, rather than with public affairs, with private individual interests, personal concerns, physical wellbeing and the mental needs and inner struggles of the self.

6. Pan-Hellenism, Pan-Europeanism and Supra-Nationalism

Firmly convinced that the role of the small political entities, the city and nation states, is played out and the traditional, inherited political frameworks are no longer capable of meeting the requirements of a new age, postclassical Greeks and post-imperialist Europeans abandon their once ardent commitment to the national or municipal bodies politic, look beyond the established boundaries of the city or nation state and start pinning their hopes on larger political and military formations.

As for ancient Greece, clear-sighted intellectuals called on the city-states already in the fourth century B.C. to abstain from conflict amongst each other and, considering their state of exhaustion after decades of war and devastation, develop a sense of pan-Hellenic unity based on the joint allegiance to Greek language, ethnicity and culture. Orators like Isocrates called on the city-states to join the Corinthian League and accept the leading role of the Macedonian kings, viewing this as the only possibility left for Greece to remain a relevant, independent actor in international affairs. In 303 B.C., Demetrius Poliorcetes drew up a constitution for a pan-Hellenic league with a shared council and president, but he saw these plans collapse after suffering military defeat against a coalition of the diadochi at the battle of Ipsus in 301 B.C. In 217 B.C. (after Rome had ended the War of the Allies), the Aitolian leader Agelaos warned the powers of Greece at a conference in Naupaktos that, unless they were to pursue a policy of pan-Hellenic unity and overcome the inherited rivalries and aversions, a dark cloud rising already in the west (i.e., either the

Romans or the Carthaginians) would soon force them into servitude and deprive all Greece of its capacity to play a relevant, autonomous role on the international political stage.

Moreover, the third century B.C. also saw the establishment of several confederations or *koina* which have been classified as the last political innovation handed to posterity by the ancient Greeks.[1] As a rule, these confederations had common treasuries, troops and federal officers like diplomats and commanders-in-chief as well as joint assemblies and federal councils authorized to decide on war and peace (some also had a uniform system of measures and weights, a common currency and joint judges, taxes and prosecution authorities). The most important of the koina were the Aitolian and Achaean leagues, the latter of which was also joined by Epirus, Athens, Sparta and Ptolemaic Egypt in 272 B.C. in an attempt to save mainland Greece from foreign (Macedonian) conquest and rule.

In the end, however, the inherited rivalries and mutual aversions between the cities and states of Hellenistic Greece proved too strong for the lasting and sustained success of any pan-Hellenic approach. In the koina, integration eventually failed as the member states refused to transfer sufficient sovereign powers, funds and military resources to the federal authorities and did not endorse the level of centralization that would have been required to ensure military efficiency and a powerful foreign policy. In fact, internal quarrel eventually caused a number of the koina including the Achaean, the Arcadian and the Thessalian leagues to disintegrate in the course of the late 3rd century B.C.[2]

Instead of pan-Hellenic unity, the inherited rivalries and the quest of the large Hellenistic monarchies (the Macedonians, the Seleucids and Ptolemaic Egypt) for supremacy over the entire *oikumene* led to a perpetuation of war among the Greeks and frustrated the original intention of averting foreign, i.e., Roman, rule. In 212 B.C., the Aitolians themselves (who, only a few years before, had warned against the imminent enslavement of all Greece by the Romans) joined forces with Rome during the Second Punic War, which they saw as an opportunity to thwart the aspirations of King Philip V

---

[1]   For a detailed analysis of the koina, cf. Hans Beck, *Polis und Koinon. Untersuchungen zur Geschichte und Struktur der griechischen Bundesstaaten im 4. Jahrhundert vor Christus*, Stuttgart 1997; A.O. Larsen, *Greek Federal States. Their Institutions and History*, Oxford 1968, 208ss.

[2]   Beck, 78ss and 132ss.

of Macedon and plunder the cities of mainland Greece. In turn, the Achaean League and Pergamum formed a coalition with Rome in the Roman–Syrian War (192–189 B.C.) against the Aitolians and the Seleucid king Antiochus III, who had tried to exploit the temporary weakness of Macedonia and expand into heartland Greece after the devastating defeat of King Philip V at the hands of the Roman legions in the Second Macedonian War.

Like many postclassical Greeks saw a need to discard the old rivalries and aversions and think along greater, pan-Hellenic lines (since the traditional political entities were considered outdated and too small), postwar Europeans established a pan-European community after World War II, which, in the longer run, was to replace and supersede the individual nation states. Just as many post-classical Greeks called for pan-Hellenic unity as the only possibility for Greece to remain a relevant actor in international affairs, postwar Europeans have sought for a joint European approach as they consider the traditional political entities inadequate and national economies too small to face the challenges of a new age.

In fact, already in the 1920s and 30s visionary European leaders like French foreign minister Aristide Briand (along with intellectuals like Thomas Mann or Stefan Zweig) nurtured the idea of a pan-European community, claiming that the nation state alone no longer had the capacity, authority and strength to secure lasting prosperity and peace.

After World War II, European integration was widely regarded as the only reasonable escape from decades of devastation caused by national selfishness, narrow-mindedness and aggression. In 1957, six European countries signed the Treaty of Rome to found the European Economic Community (EEC). In 1967 and 1993 respectively, the latter was transformed into the European Community (EC) and the European Union (EU), each of these transformations coming along with increased levels of political, financial and economic integration. As the Union grew to encompass eventually 28 member states in 2012 in a process of progressive enlargement, Europe has seen the establishment of the common market, the borderless Schengen Area, the institution of the EU Council and EU Commission president, the European Central Bank, the EU Parliament, the European Court of

Justice, and finally, the appointment of a High Representative for Security Policy and Foreign Affairs.

Envisaging the establishment of a United States of Europe (as a political union or federation), the EU elites reiterate that, on their own, the nation states of Europe have become unable to play a significant role and bring their influence to bear on the global political stage. Persistently, they aim to convince their citizens to consider themselves no longer as members of an individual nation state and to adopt a joint European identity, warning that — without the European Union — the nations of Europe would fall victim to the whims of foreign interest and soon find themselves at the hands and mercy of outside political and economic powers.

If the structural analogy between ancient Greece and modern Europe is correct, however, the eventual failure of the Greeks to cast aside the inherited aversions and embrace a new, pan-Hellenic approach does not bode well either for Europe's pursuit of a joint, pan-European future: judging by what happened to the pan-Hellenic efforts and aspirations of ancient Greece, there is much to suggest that rivalry and mutual dislike amongst the nations of Europe and the sustained predominance of national self-interest will eventually prevent the establishment of lasting unity and concord or, in other words: that the enduring differences and divides among the nations of Europe and the sore lack of togetherness within Europe are likely to impede the efficient integration of Europe and hamper its capacity of pursuing effective (common) defense and foreign policies or developing a forceful and efficient set of common political institutions. In fact, attitudes to the EU project have deteriorated steadily and centrifugal powers have increased progressively in recent years, strikingly reflected in the fact that French, Dutch and Irish voters all turned down the EU constitution or the Treaty of Lisbon in a series of national referenda in 2005–2008. While significant parts of the British public look determined to leave the EU altogether and countries like Poland, Sweden or Denmark refuse joining the single European currency system, the process of decision-making in Europe remains agonizingly slow and cumbersome in consideration of veto powers and the need for unanimous votes in a manner structurally similar to the consistently inefficient internal organization of the ancient *koina* and the lasting inability of the Greeks to speak with one voice on the international political stage.

As a matter of fact, national resentment and mutual dislike among the nations of Europe have sprung up again especially since the sovereign debt crisis hit the continent in 2009 and widespread reluctance resulted to provide financial solidarity within Europe. While mass-market newspapers in Germany take pleasure in mocking the Southern Europeans as inert, fraudulent and lazy, Greek demonstrators repeatedly depicted the German chancellor and finance minister in SS uniforms. A Eurobarometer survey conducted across Europe in the spring of 2012 revealed that the share of those having a positive image of the European Union was down to a record low of 31%, while 60% said they had no trust whatsoever in the EU project. With national resentment on the rise and spectacular electoral success achieved by euroskeptic parties (like UKIP in Great Britain, the True Finns in Finland, the Sweden Democrats in Sweden, the FPÖ in Austria or the Five Star Movement in Italy), the future of the European project is anything but certain and parallels suggest themselves with the eventual fate of the pan-Hellenic aspirations and federalist experiments in Hellenistic Greece.

Besides the quest for pan-European unity and community, another striking fact is that the Europeans tend to be substantially more prepared than the Americans to support international organizations such as the United Nations, the International Criminal Court or the International War Crimes Tribunal. Whereas the Americans tend to be skeptical in principle about the very concept of multilateralism, most Europeans have subscribed to a "postnational model of peace, prosperity, social justice, ecological virtue and international cooperation."[1] Considering the ostentatious patriotism of flag-saluting Americans (or American schoolchildren starting the day by pledging allegiance to the nation) as outdated or embarrassing, many present-day Europeans believe that national confines and boundaries ought to be overcome in favor of international cooperation and supranational regulation. By contrast, most Americans are skeptical in principle about any outside interference into their own constitutional framework or any transfer of sovereign powers from their own political institutions to supranational levels.

---

[1] Walter Laqueur, *After the Fall. The End of the European Dream and the Decline of a Continent*, New York 2012, 3/261ss.

In fact, the United Nations is viewed by many Americans with distaste or contempt, and the U.S. explicitly suspended its payments to the United Nations in 1996 at the instigation of Congress. While the Europeans tend to be willing and prepared to delegate rights and powers from their national political frameworks to larger, international entities, the U.S. remains reluctant to support supranational organizations and agreements like the International Land Mine Treaty, the Kyoto Protocol or the UN Chemical Weapons Convention — regarding such agreements and institutions as bothersome constraints of its national sovereignty and undue limits to its own room for maneuver. Perhaps most ostensibly, this was reflected in the fact that the United States government not only ignored a verdict from the International Court of Justice in The Hague denouncing their use of mines in Nicaraguan ports in 1986 but virtually threatened to use military force against the court as an institution in order to free any American citizen held by that court should the judges dare to capture, detain or imprison a U.S. officer or soldier.[1]

As a general fact, the disparity of attitudes and values between modern Europeans and Americans bears a strong resemblance to the conflicting mentalities of the ancient Greeks and Romans respectively in the late Hellenistic age. For whereas Romans of the second century B.C. remained intensely committed to their homeland and tied to their national institutions and ways of life, the Greeks tended to be convinced that national and municipal boundaries ought to be overcome, as they readily embraced cosmopolitan views and focused on the universal nature of man rather than maintaining the former commitment to the old, municipal institutions and conventions of the city-state. Strongly contrasting with the essentially national spirit of Rome, postclassical Greek philosophy championed the cause of universal philanthropy and concentrated on the human being as such, liberated from traditional, national and municipal bonds for the sake of all-embracing brotherhood in a global universal community. As a consequence, it was still good custom for a Roman politician of the second century B.C. to dissociate himself from Greek universalism and emphasize his lasting commitment to the national spirit of Rome.

---

[1] Originally introduced by Senator Jesse Helms, the American Services Members' Protection Act or so-called *The Hague Invasion Act* was passed by Congress and signed into law by George W. Bush in 2002.

Quite similarly, we still find an unshakeable sense of loyalty to the nation, its values, interests and actions in America, which has become virtually unthinkable in contemporary Europe. Like pan-Hellenism and cosmopolitanism in the case of ancient Greece, the pan-European aspirations and the willingness among Europeans to transfer sovereign powers to supranational organizations are indications of alienation from the national political frameworks and a lack of confidence in the power and authority of the nation state.

Like the sense of bewilderment among many present-day Europeans at the unquestioned patriotism of modern Americans, the ancient Greek rejection of Rome's essentially national spirit in favor of universalism, cosmopolitanism and supranational cooperation reflects the fact that postclassical Greeks and Europeans have ceased believing in the capacity and strength of their inherited institutions and bodies politic and hence seek for an exit from traditional, national history. By contrast, the Romans and Americans know (or knew) that their constitutional frameworks and national bodies politic are still young and vigorous and hence deserve unquestioned loyalty and commitment. Having trust and confidence in the sustained capacity of their constitutional systems and the lasting authority of their national political frameworks, they remain committed to their national bodies politic, disapprove the transfer of sovereign powers to foreign entities and levels and remain essentially hostile to any preference for universal humanity over patriotism and national allegiance.

7. How the Greeks Saw the Romans and Europeans See the Americans

On the one hand, there has always been a strong sense of admiration among the ancient Greeks and modern Europeans for the superior military might, political skill, economic efficiency and technological capability of the Romans and Americans respectively — as well as, of course, for their monumental architecture, which let the Greek poleis look as humble in comparison to Rome as the cities of Europe do in comparison to the skylines and urban landscapes of New York and other major American cities. (After all, the pragmatic business-minded spirit of the Romans and Americans represents the consistent continuation of trends in Hellenistic Greece and 19th century Europe, which were already periods shaped by technical and scientific rationality. Generally, the focus of the high cultural formations gradually tends to shift from heroism and war in the early period to science and technology in the medium phase and finally industry, commerce and trade in the later stages, as the spirit of rationality turns increasingly *instrumental*). On the other hand, however, there has also been a strong notion of contempt and disdain for the Romans and Americans respectively among the ancient Greeks and modern Europeans.

In particular, the Hellenistic Greeks tended to despise the rudeness of the Romans, their rapacity and the cruelty of their games. By contrast to the harshness with which the Romans treated their enemies, and also their own legionaries and soldiers (including the practice of decimation, where one out of ten soldiers who had participated in a rebellion or other major crime had to be executed by his own comrades, often through stoning or clubbing), Stoic philosophy nurtured the philanthropic vision that all men should act as brothers and everybody deserved humane treatment irrespective of nationality, status and rank.

In a basically similar manner, many Europeans tend to be appalled at Americans' insistence on the death penalty, the right to bear arms, the appreciation of the gun as a symbol of freedom, and high levels of violence and crime. They eagerly criticize the American inclination to military intervention and war and deplore the reluctance of the United States to follow Europe's disposition towards pacifism, diplomacy, environmental consideration and restraint in the use of military force.

Moreover, both the Hellenistic Greeks and present-day Europeans challenged (or challenge) the notoriously good conscience of the Romans and Americans, as was reflected in Cicero's assertion that all wars waged by Rome had been essentially just, that Roman rule was only for the benefit of those subjected and that it was Rome's inherent mission to bring peace, order and justice to all parts of what was regarded as the civilized world. In modern times, the Americans insist, along very similar lines, that the blessed mission of the United States is to be a champion of liberty, forge a new global order as the "leader of the free world" and share its vision of freedom and democracy with all nations of the globe. Both the ancient Romans and the modern Americans have been keen to reiterate that they are the greatest, freest, most enlightened and most virtuous people in the world, indispensable as a guarantor of international stability and prosperity — or even, in the case of America, a light to the world, a model for all nations and encouragement of mankind, chosen by providence to show the world the way to freedom. What the Romans and Americans share, much to the displeasure of the Greeks and Europeans, is a deep sense of superiority, which lets their ways, actions and wars appear as a struggle of justice against injustice or good versus evil (and indeed, the ancient Romans and present-day Americans do have a point in claiming that, without their presence and contribution, the world would soon sink into barbarism, tyranny and chaos.)

Whereas the Romans and Americans tend to believe that any political order which they establish and impose on others is essentially just and that every power opposing them is basically illegitimate (so that the use of military force is seen as a way to express Rome's and America's commitment to the common weal of the world), the Greeks and Europeans respectively have tended to consider the unshakably good conscience of the Romans and Americans as either plain hypocrisy or as the blatant attempt to embellish an imperialistic urge for power. Challenging the firm belief of the Romans and Americans that their wars are axiomatically legitimate as *bella iusta* or wars for the sake of democracy, freedom and human rights, the Greeks and Europeans tend to denounce the superpower's moral self-assuredness as Roman "*superbia*" or American "presumption."

Both Greek philosophers of the second century B.C. and 20th century European intellectuals have been quick to criticize the Romans and Americans respectively as brutal, hypocritical and ruthless. When an embassy of Greek philosophers visited Rome in 155 B.C., Carneades the Skeptic delivered a speech in which he challenged Rome's alleged moral superiority and claimed that, in reality, Roman rule was not based on justice but on violence, rapacity and exploitation. (This prompted Cato the Elder to file a senatorial motion to send the embassy back to Greece before the philosophers had the opportunity to confuse or spoil the youth of Rome.) In modern times, European intellectuals have been quick to accuse the Americans of vulgarity, unscrupulous materialism and a relentless thirst for profit, which they claim are the true motivations of any U.S. policy, only glossed over by the recurring litanies of democracy and liberation.

"The stereotype of the ugly American — voracious, preachy, mercenary, and bombastically chauvinist has always been popular in Europe" since the late 19th century, Simon Schama noted in an essay on *The Unloved American* in 2003.[1] Even more outspokenly, the German journalist Rolf Winter held in an extensive essay, published in 1989 under the telling title of *Ami Go Home. Farewell to a Violent Country*: "The vulgarly capitalist United States have become what they are today through violence ... Habitually incapable of peace, they are forever on a crusade ... Barely any other Western civilization is more unsavory than the one created by the Americans. Barely any other country is haunted by as much ordinary racism, violent crime, unrestrained greed

---

[1] Simon Schama, "The Unloved American. Two Centuries of Alienating Europe," in: *The New Yorker*, 10 March 2003.

and corruption. Nowhere else is the fight for profit and economic success waged in more inhumane and cold-blooded ways. Nowhere else are possession and wealth more adored as the only purposes in life, and poverty more deserted and despised."[1]

In the eyes of many Europeans, the American insistence on liberty, democracy and (Christian) piety is only deception and fraud, and America's moral rhetoric only serves to cover self-interest and financial greed, as they accuse the Americans of threatening traditional European values with a commercialized culture of vulgar entertainment, economic recklessness and genetically engineered food. Moreover, the Europeans also tend to contrast with the Americans in having a consistently bad conscience, readily denouncing the wickedness of their violent and imperialist past. Anxious to avoid relapsing into "eurocentrism" and eagerly taking the blame for the misdeeds of their ancestors, they consider the righteousness, unshakeable self-confidence and self-assuredness displayed by the Americans to be expressions of hypocrisy, moral deficiency and double standards.

In historical perspective, however, the complacency and alleged moral superiority of the Greeks and Europeans respectively and their pride in being more civilized, peaceful and considerate than the Romans and Americans may, after all, only reflect a lack of the political qualities and mental constitution which it takes to assert oneself in international politics and on the global political stage (or, in other words, indicate a loss of political vitality, energy and vigor). Just as many cities of Greece were pleasant, safe and prosperous places to live but were no longer geopolitical actors or makers of history during the age of Roman supremacy in the second century B.C., present-day Europe is certainly a less dangerous and more secure place to live than most parts of the United States[2] while, at the same time, its nations have become widely irrelevant in military and geopolitical terms. Whereas post-heroic notions of universal peace and individual

---

[1]   Rolf Winter, *Ami Go Home. Plädoyer für den Abschied von einem gewalttätigen Land*, Hamburg 1989, 32.

[2]   According to statistics, the number of people killed by guns in the U.S. is eight times that of Great Britain and 24 times that of Switzerland. In terms of rape and robbery, the relations between Europe and the U.S. are 1:7 and 1:5 respectively. Figures published on the website of the International Centre for Prison Studies show the United States had a prison population rate of 716 per 100,000 of the national population (as of 2013), while the corresponding figures were 82 for the Netherlands, 79 for Germany and 67 for Sweden.

self-realization — combined with a consistently bad conscience about one's own violent and bellicose past — prevail in postclassical Greece and Europe respectively, one still finds a determination not to question the legitimacy of the nation, its actions and institutions in modern America and ancient Rome.

At the end of the day, the way in which the Hellenistic Greeks and post-imperialist Europeans morally condemn the rougher socio-cultural practices and powerful foreign policies pursued by Rome and the United States may only reflect the fact that they have ceased believing in themselves as having the potential to be makers of history and forceful actors of international politics, as they no longer have confidence in the lasting authority, potency and capacity of their national bodies politic. As a result, they have come to lack the political properties and mental constitution required from those wishing to make an impact on the course of global history, and tend to be suspicious of the qualities and attributes, which it takes to do so. Like the Hellenistic Greeks in the face of Rome, present-day Europeans feel uneasy and uncomfortable when faced with the attitudes of a nation (i.e., the Americans) which is still ready to impose its will on others and assert itself on the global political scale, and still harbors a sense of national greatness and glory. By contrast, the unshakably good confidence of the Romans and Americans, their pride in military achievements, their political assertiveness and their conviction of having a mission for the rest of the world are manifestations of belief in the potency and vigor of the nation and of an unbroken, unquestioned allegiance to its inherited political and constitutional frameworks, which is no longer to be found in postclassical Greece and Europe respectively. While the loss of patriotic conviction and the disdain of power politics among the Greeks and Europeans indicate a lack of trust in the sustained capacity of their inherited (municipal or national) constitutional frameworks, the Romans and Americans maintain the ambition to make history, use military force if necessary to assert themselves on the global political stage and preserve the qualities required for shaping the world by political means, as they still have confidence and trust in the lasting vitality of their nations and the sustained authority of their national bodies politic.

8. How the Romans Saw the Greeks and Americans See the Europeans

Though borrowing heavily, for long periods of time, from Greek and European culture and thought, the Romans and Americans have tended to look with disdain at the military weakness, political impotence and moral permissiveness of the (postclassical) Greeks and Europeans respectively. While many educated Greeks considered the Romans hypocritical and prudish, conservative Romans warned of abandoning traditional Roman values and the moral strictness of the res publica Romana in favor of Greek permissiveness, libertinism and leisure.

Above all others, Cato the Elder put up resistance to the ascendancy of Philhellenism and opposed the steadily rising influence of Greek literature, philosophy, drama and art among Rome's upper class. Time and again, he warned his fellow countrymen not to let Greek leisure, refined taste, competitive athletics and dramatic art prevail over Rome's inherited culture of agricultural industry, political eloquence and military bravery. In particular, Cato objected to the skepticism and relativism of the Greek philosophers, emphasizing the fundamental opposition between the *mos maiorum* (shaped by values like endurance, frugality, simplicity, bravery, discipline, perseverance, modesty and industry) and Greek philosophical 'humanitas,' whose influence had begun to steadily increase since the start of the second century B.C. For long periods of time, the Romans sought to avoid infiltration by the *otium Graecum*, anxious to prevent Rome's military tradition, rustic values, sanctity of family life and allegiance to the institutions of the state from being undermined by Greek universalism, effeminacy and weakness.

Repeatedly, laws were passed against the Greek culture of luxury, permissiveness, idleness and theatrical amusement. In 186 B.C., the cult of the Bacchanalia was prohibited in Rome in an attempt to defend the morality and religious practice of the Roman people against the indiscipline, sexual debauchery and licentiousness of the Hellenistic cults.[1] In 173 B.C., the Epicurean philosophers Alkaios and Philiskos were expelled from the city as "teachers of pleasure," considered as threatening the national spirit of Rome with intoxication by Greek skepticism, effeminacy and doubt. Still in 155 B.C., the pontifex maximus Scipio Nasica ordered the city's first two stone-built theaters to be demolished in an attempt to prevent Greek dramatic art from taking root and establishing itself on a permanent basis inside the confines of the city of Rome.

Like the Romans who warned of Greek effeminacy and decadence in the third and second century B.C., Americans tend to be skeptical about European libertinism, hedonism and sexual permissiveness, while the Europeans complain of a typically American prudishness. Moreover, the United States persistently defends its culture of harsh, unfettered capitalism and entrepreneurial openness to new technology against the softer, more cautious European system of social welfare, security and restraint. As it was still recommendable for a Roman politician to dissociate himself from Greek decadence and weakness and not to admit his reliance on advice from the Greek intellectuals, the *Graeculi* in the second century B.C., U.S. presidential candidates are well advised to tell their electorate that they do not wish to follow the morally decadent and economically deplorable ways of Europe.[2] Like the Romans, who tended to see Greek philosophical sophistication as a threat to national loyalty (which, among other things, caused the Senate to order the public burning of the Pythagorean "books of numa" in 181 B.C. and led to the repeated eviction or prohibition of Greek philosophical schools), many Americans tend to be suspicious of European intellectual obfuscations.

---

[1]   Eric Orlin, "Urban Religion in the Middle and Late Republic," in: Jörg Rüpke (ed.), *A Companion to Roman Religion*, Malden/Mass 2007, 58-70, 64.
[2]   Madden, 155. In fact, Thomas Jefferson was already calling the Europeans "wimps" and "weaklings" in the early years of the 19th century.

At the same time, conflicting attitudes also extend to the area of social and family values: amongst most Romans, the Greek culture of pederastic relationships with minors and naked physical exercise was considered intolerable and obscene, while today many Americans are skeptical about European moral and sexual permissiveness. Generally, the family was still held in high esteem as the fundamental societal unit by the Romans, while individualism and personal autonomy had already become the guiding principles of Hellenistic society and socio-philosophical thought. The role of the woman was still defined more conservatively in Rome than in the "progressive" Hellenistic east; the ideal of a Roman upper-class woman still was the domestic working of wool and confinement to the house, and women's emancipation only began after the collapse of the republic and the establishment of the empire during the first century B.C. Similarly, the general perception of the woman's role in society is still more traditional in the United States than in most parts of Europe.

In major sections of American society, the role model for a woman is still the housewife and stay-at-home mother who focuses on raising her children and does not resort to institutional childcare services along European habits and lines. Generally speaking, commonplace Americans are still more committed to traditional family values and more skeptical about divorce, abortion and gay marriage than commonplace Europeans. In Rome and America alike, the willingness to preserve traditional values and the resolution not to embrace post heroic, posthistorical notions of indulgence and permissiveness reflects the determination to uphold the qualities required to maintain the nation's political potency and vigor. In both cases, the superpower refuses to allow the strengths and qualities to be undermined by Greek and European softness, cautiousness and permissiveness, a refusal which helps it to fulfill its role as a hegemonic actor of global politics and powerful force of international history.

Only since the late first century B.C. and early first century A.D., when the republican institutions had eventually disintegrated and collapsed, did Roman poetry begin promoting a post-heroic life of love, peace and comfort, praising the modest pleasures of rural life, as a new cultural paradigm suggested to withdraw from politics and public life in favor of private happiness, personal emotion and harmony with nature. The prose and drama of the late republic and early empire, as epitomized most prominently by Virgil, no longer occupied itself with the political reality and public life of Rome but rather with mythology, the longing for peace, the pleasures of love and modest life on a small landed estate.

At the same time, poetry and theater came to be dominated by eroticism, mythology and the post-heroic, post-political values of the *ars amatoria*, as represented by Ovid, Propertius, Tibullus and Catullus, whose poems focused on love, intimacy, marital life and sexual relations. Not by accident did Greek "post heroic" ideas of universal peace, love and unity of mankind only prevail in Rome after the collapse of the republic and the establishment of the empire in the first century A.D., when a national body politic and constitutional framework no longer existed that was to be bolstered by civic discipline and morale. It was only in those days as well that "philanthropic" laws were passed against the harsh treatment of slaves and that Nero sought to replace the inherited national spirit and military tradition of Rome with a "Greek" culture of theater, music, amusement and dance.

As the harshness, rigidity and assertiveness once required from Roman citizens for maintaining the strength of the republic and the vigor of its national institutions was no longer in demand and universal (philanthropic) rule of the entire world became the order of the day, the time had come for Rome to embrace and surrender to the post-heroic notions, post-political values and universalistic principles of Hellenistic Greece. Looking at present-day America, the conclusion hence to be drawn from historical analogy would be that, for as long as America insists on its exceptional character, retains its national spirit and does not surrender to the post-political attitudes and post-heroic notions, which many Europeans would like it to embrace (including the abandonment of the death penalty and the abolition of the right to bear arms), the transformation of the American republic into an empire proper exercising universal (philanthropic) control of all mankind and imperial, cosmopolitan rule — and thus no longer relying on the maintenance of civic virtue and a resolute patriotic spirit — still appears to be a substantially distant perspective.

9. American Puritanism and Roman Religiousness

The strong religious sentiment and puritan spirit of America, which meets with so much bewilderment and alienation among many present-day Europeans, bear strong resemblance as well to the attitudes of the ancient Romans who, for long periods of time, remained intensely committed to traditional religion, as Roman politics was factually inseparable from religious practice. Indeed, the entirety of Roman life was embedded in civic religion, as the Romans stood in continuous contact with divine force through augurs and auspices, and Roman consuls prayed for support from the gods ahead of every major undertaking or campaign. Auspication by the presiding magistrate and interpretation of the auspices by the augurs' college preceded every important decision to be taken on behalf of the state including the passing of laws and the holding of elections. Throughout Rome's republican history, priests would study the flight of living birds and examine the entrails of dead sheep to predict victory or defeat. Prior to every departure for war or in the rare event of military defeat, the entire adult population was encouraged to pray in the temples and implore mercy from the gods.

Generally, strong ties were in place between religion and the state, whose magistrates administered the official cults (such as the cult of the Vestals) and superintended the course of religious practice. For long periods of time, the Romans rejected the enlightenment, atheism and agnosticism, which had spread so widely and prevailed so strongly in the Hellenistic world. Whereas confidence in the traditional divinities and municipal cults of the city-state had long declined in the Hellenistic context, and religious belief had given way to sensualistic and materialistic thought, as a spirit of rationality viewed the gods as mere illusions and human creations, the Romans still adhered to their inherited gods, closely tied as they were to the soil, the house (the lares and penates) and the institutions of the state.

While Roman politics remained intensely committed to inherited religion, the enlightened Greek Polybius voiced astonishment at the extensive role still played by religious practice in the political and private life of Rome, referring at one point to the "almost superstitious fear of the gods that forms the basis of the Roman state."[1] In fact, the civic theology of Rome was consistently administered and supervised by the state, which appointed the priests and took charge of public cultic performance by the pontifices, the augural college, the arval brethren, the sacerdotes and the flamines. Every establishment of a new cult and every building of a new temple inside the boundaries of the city required permission from the people and senate of Rome.[2] As Eric Orlin has pointed out, Roman religion was tightly interwoven with political authority, as the senate governed and controlled the priestly colleges (including the pontiffs, the augurs and the decemviri).[3]

According to Orlin, the "primary purpose of public religion was to protect and enhance the community of the Romans ... The welfare of the city and its inhabitants was ensured through religious rituals, by which the Romans attempted to secure the good will of the gods."[4] In fact, it was even good custom to stop or suspend political undertakings "because an official with religious authority had observed signs that the gods were unfavorable to the conduct of public business."[5] Similar to modern Americans, the Romans therefore claimed to be (in the words of Cicero) "the most pious of all nations"[6], as religion had to be practiced in public, secret cults were banned, and the pontifex maximus (or high priest) — who oversaw the city's religious ceremonies and life — was an official government position. By contrast, very few Greeks still took the gods seriously

---

[1] Quoted in Hans-Josef Klauck, *The Religious Context of Early Christianity. A Guide to Greco-Roman Religions*, London/New York 2003, 422.
[2] Jörg Rüpke, "Roman Religion," in: Flower (ed.), 179-195, 191.
[3] Orlin, 59.
[4] Eric Orlin, 58.
[5] Orlin, 58, 66.
[6] Orlin, 58.

in the second century B.C., when they had come to live in a largely postreligious world of skepticism, sensualism and materialism, as is the case today with most 21st century Europeans.

Like many Hellenistic Greeks facing the vibrant religious life of Rome, postwar Europeans tend to feel bewildered at the strong religious sentiment in the United States and its symbiotic interconnection of religious energy, power politics, capitalist impetus and consumer culture. In particular, many Europeans are estranged by the fact that mega churches in the United States have thousands or tens of thousands of weekend service attendees, that Christian fundamentalism is a mainstream force in American politics and that religious TV and radio broadcasters play a massive role in the U.S. media landscape. In fact, Christian fundamentalism and Christian schooling are endorsed by substantial sections of the U.S. population, as one in three Americans consider themselves to be reborn Christians and 25% of those entitled to vote view themselves as right-wing evangelicals.

Whereas atheism and agnosticism progressively prevail in Europe, 89% of all Americans consider themselves religious and 78% say that praying represents an important element of their daily lives (according to a survey conducted in 2013). By contrast, fewer than one in ten attend church at least once a month in Britain, the Netherlands, Germany and Sweden.[1]

From the Founding Fathers till today, the United States has perceived itself as "God's own country" and agent in the world, a New Jerusalem and nation blessed by god, whose presidents insist on acting in the name of the Lord.

Throughout U.S. history, presidents and congressmen have been anxious to present themselves as God-fearing patriots and servants of the nation — in which they claim that god has implanted visions of liberty and freedom, providing it with unique favors and distinguishing it from all other nations of the world. "Our faith teaches that there is no safer reliance than on the God of our fathers, who has so singularly favored the American people in every national trial, and who will not forsake us so long as we obey His commandments and walk humbly in His footsteps," declared William McKinley, 25th president of the United States, in his 1897 inaugural address.[2]

---

[1] Ferguson, 236.
[2] http://www.god-and-country.info/WMcKinley.html

A generation later, Senator Albert Beveridge claimed in a speech — highlighting the intrinsic relationship being in place in the United States between religion (or religious belief) and national self-conception — that god himself had made the Americans "the master organizers of the world, to establish a system where otherwise chaos reigns.... Of all our race, he has marked the American people as His chosen nation to finally lead in the regeneration of the world. This is the divine mission of America, and it holds for us all the profit, all the glory, all the happiness possible to man."[1]

As for the reasons and historical significance of lasting religious commitment among the ancient Romans and modern Americans, an important factor appears to lie in the conviction already of the founding fathers that only those believing in God can be good citizens and that free political institutions cannot function without the religious commitment of its citizens. Similar to the ancient Romans, the founding fathers believed that the lastingness and durability of republican institutions required the citizens to believe in god and that a republican constitution could only work sustainably with a moral and religious people.[2]

At the end of the day, it seems as though the intrinsic connection between lasting religious commitment on the one hand and durable political institutions on the other rests on the fact that any enduring allegiance to a constitution and body politic requires the attachment to institutions outlasting the life of the individual, as they originate from a distant past and are poised to continue existing beyond the lifetime of the individual. As a consequence, any lasting reverence for a constitutional framework and body politic, as it was (or is) so typical of modern America and ancient Rome and lets the Romans and Americans stand out from Greece and Europe respectively, can only be provided by a people committed to the idea of authority, i.e., the unquestioned acknowledgement of entities or institutions with roots and origins in the distant past. Considering the circumstance, however, that the basic source of authority is and always was religious belief, an intrinsic relationship is in place indeed between the Romans' and Americans' adherence to religion and the exceptional vigor and lastingness of their constitutional frameworks and bodies politic. The exceptional constitutional commitment of modern

---

[1] Congressional Record of the 56th Congress, 1st Session, 704-712.
[2] Cf. Madden, 53.

America and ancient Rome, which differs so substantially from the political conditions of postclassical Greece and Europe respectively, suggests that lasting commitment to the authority of a body politic is effectively inseparable in the final analysis from enduring allegiance to the authority of divine force.

In *On Revolution*, Hannah Arendt extensively discusses the history of the American Revolution, whose "chief task turned out to be the establishment not of power, but of authority,"[1] and places emphasis on the fundamental interrelatedness of authority, tradition and the act of foundation (of a republic) in modern America and ancient Rome.[2] At the same time, it was a firm conviction shared already by the founding fathers that the lasting acknowledgement of the act of foundation as a source of authority could not possibly function with an essentially irreligious people of non-believers who axiomatically refuse to respect and revere transcendent divine force — and are hence insusceptible to the basic religious origins and foundations of the concept of authority.

By contrast to the Romans, the educated elites of Hellenistic Greece tended to be atheistic or agnostic ever since the third century B.C., sharing the belief of Epicurus that man must determine his own fate and live on his own responsibility without relying on support or orientation from supernatural religious powers. Similarly, it has become a commonplace view in present-day Europe that individuals and societies should autonomously shape their own destinies or lives without resorting to the forces of religion and a general moral system underpinned by religious belief.

Given the intrinsic relationship discussed above between lasting religious belief and enduring political vigor, the rise of religious skepticism and post-religious sentiment in postclassical Greece and post-imperialist Europe provides indication that, in these parts of the world, the very idea of authority has been abandoned, which constitutes a basic prerequisite of lasting allegiance to political frameworks and reverence for national constitutional foundations.

In postclassical Greece and post-imperialist Europe, the loss of confidence in religious authority correlates with a loss of confidence in the national constitutional frameworks or bodies politic and in the city or nations states' capacity of being relevant actors in international affairs and forceful makers of human history. In both antiquity and in

---

[1] Hannah Arendt, *On Revolution*, London 1990, 178.
[2] Arendt, On Revolution, 199.

the modern world, it looks as though an inseparable correlation is in place between the level of religiousness within a society and the level of belief in the power and capacity of the nation (or the lasting authority of national political institutions). In a way, the Romans and Americans still consider(ed) their nations and bodies politic as sacred entities worthy of God's grace, attention and concern — a confidence, which is no longer to be found among the postclassical Greeks and Europeans. By implication, however, this also indicates that, for as long as religious indifference and skepticism do not rise in the United States and Americans do not turn their backs on religious belief, the American constitution and the institutional fabrics of the American republic will continue to rest on rather solid foundations.

10. Radical Ideology and Utopian Vision

At a certain point during the transition from classical to postclassical Greece and from classical to postclassical Europe, forces of radical ideology arose that refused paying any allegiance to the city or nation state, and denied the need for a state or government altogether. Early Stoicism, Cynicism and Epicureanism all devoted themselves to the cause of cosmopolitanism and universal human equality, as they focused on the human being *in abstracto*, absolved from municipal or national bonds (since all humans were regarded as sharing the same rational capacity and being subject to the same moral and natural law).[1]

Conceiving the ideal human community as global, cosmopolitan and universal, they saw the human being no longer as a member or citizen of a particular city-state. Zeno, the founder of the Stoic school who taught in Athens from around 300 B.C., envisaged a communist society and cosmopolitan community of perfect harmony and concord, in which all inherited distinctions between citizens, strangers and slaves were cast aside.[2]

In particular, Epicurus and the Cynics committed themselves to strict abstention from any political activity, fiercely refusing to get involved in municipal politics or show loyalty to the institutions of the city-state. The home of the cynic was considered to be no-where and everywhere in

---

[1] Robert W. Sharples, *Stoics, Epicureans and Skeptics. An Introduction to Hellenistic Philosophy*, New York 1996, 235; Long, From Epicurus to Epictetus, 346.
[2] Long, From Epicurus to Epictetus, 346.

the world, as he strove to live the homeless life of a vagabond without a city, country, home or place of his own (a-polis, a-oikos[1]). Explicitly, freedom was defined as being a citizen of the universe, not belonging to any polis or nation, a stranger in all parts and places of the world who rejected the conventional separation of human beings by nations, cities or states.[2] In fact, Epicurus claimed that, if all men were to become Epicureans, laws and states would no longer be required, as people would live in universal harmony, justice and concord, unbothered by the disturbances of politics and the constraints of law.[3]

Conjuring an Epicurean millennium, Diogenes of Oenoanda predicted that "truly the life of the gods will pass to human beings. For everything will be full of justice and mutual friendship, and there will come to be no need of city-walls or laws ..."[4] Cynicism and Epicureanism both called on the individual to dismiss traditional social bonds or family obligations and do without possession, fostering the principles of autarky, subjective autonomy and radical self-sufficiency. Shaping his life in self-determination, the individual should not allow himself to be dependent on earthly matters and outside entities — which were considered alien to his true human essence — but live in greatest possible isolation from the matters of the world.

The Stoic ideal of the *oikeosis* conceived the human community as one big cosmopolitan family or oikos, serving the purposes of self-preservation, physical wellbeing and sustained peace of mind without the need for a public or political sphere. Instead of being committed to the inherited institutional structures of the body politic and acting in concert with one's fellow-citizens, the individual was to live in concealment (seclusion) and attend to matters of the self, fully concentrating on the inwardness of his mental operations (in pursuance of harmony with reason) and the immediacy of his bodily functions and physical needs from sexuality and digestion to

---

[1] Cf. Robert Bracht Branham / Marie-Odile Goulet-Cazé (eds.), *The Cynics. The Cynic Movement in Antiquity and its Legacy*, Berkeley et al. 1996, Introduction, 1-27, 24; M.O. Goulet-Cazé, "Religion and the Early Cynics," in: Branham / Goulet-Cazé, 47-80; John L. Moles, "Cynic Cosmopolitanism," in: Branham / Goulet-Cazé, 105-120, who especially stresses the Cynic view of social and family obligations as obstacles to individual freedom.
[2] John L. Moles, Cynic Cosmopolitanism, 109s.
[3] Robert W. Sharples, "Philosophy for Life," in: Bugh (ed.), 223-240, 231.
[4] As quoted by Long, From Epicurus to Epictetus, 198.

hygiene and nutrition. Steeped in radical individualism,[1] the cynics virtually lived in the streets, keen to satisfy only their natural needs with no possession except for the hiking stick and the begging cup in a state of greatest possible independence of all worldly entities, bonds and affairs. Disregarding moral conventions and ridiculing national authorities, they concentrated on the immediacy of their bodily functions, lived for the day and indulged in the public display of sexuality, urination and dejection.

One of the most striking manifestations of postclassical Greek philosophy's turn towards the immediacy of physical, bodily (or natural) functions certainly is to be seen in the demand by Zeno, the founder of the Stoic school, that human beings should not live together in a polis (i.e., according to the classical definition of man as a *zoon politicon*) but rather in accordance with nature "like a herd of cattle grazing harmonically on the same pasture and nourished by one and the same natural law."[2] According to Zeno, humans ought to view the animal kingdom as a role model for life in harmony with nature and hence subscribe to "only one way of life and order like herds of animals do on their meadows."[3]

On similar grounds, Epicurus claimed that humans should in fact envy (and try to emulate) the animals, as they were able to live in self-sufficiency, without fear of death, fear of the gods and the burden of worldly concerns. The famous Cynic Diogenes of Sinope held that man should live "like a dog" or "in a dog-like way."[4] In fact, the very name of the Cynic movement was derived from *kyon* and *kynikos*, i.e., the ancient Greek equivalents for dog and dog-like.

Moreover, the third and second century B.C. also was the heyday of ancient Greek utopian thought: Euhemerus of Messene, who served with king Cassander of Macedon from 311 to 298 B.C., fancied a fictional, utopian city on an island, where private property was absent and any produce was equitably divided among those who worked for the benefit of a solidly united community, cosmopolitically embracing

---

[1] A.A. Long, "The Socratic Tradition. Diogenes, Crates and Hellenistic Ethics," in: Branham/Goulet-Cazé, 28-46, 40ss.
[2] A.A. Long/ D.N. Sedley, *The Hellenistic Philosophers (German version)*, Stuttgart/Weimar 2000, 512s, Andrew Erskine, *The Hellenistic Stoa, Political Thought and Action*, London 1990, John Ferguson, *Utopias of the Classical World*, London 1975, 113.
[3] Mossé, 188.
[4] Goulet-Cazé, "Religion and the Early Cynics," in: Branham/Goulet-Cazé (eds.), 47-80, 62, Moles, 112.

customs and traditions from all parts of the world.[1] A few years later, Cassander's brother Alexarchus tried to turn fiction into reality by founding the communist republic of Ouranopolis (Heaven City) on the Athos peninsula in northern Greece. The philosopher Iambulus likewise projected a utopian society, in which civil concord was considered the highest value, work was performed by all members of the community in rotation, and people did not spend their time on political debating but whiled away their lives in enjoyment of the many things which nature has to offer for human sustenance and delight.[2] In 133–131 B.C., Eumenes III of Pergamum finally founded Heliopolis, a utopian city where all men and women were supposed to be free and universal liberation was promised to serfs and slaves.

In modern Europe, we can see similar developments during the second half of the 19th century with the emergence of socialism, communism and anarchism, which argued for the state to die off and the political (or genuinely public) sphere to be abolished in favor of a global cosmopolitan community. For the adherents of socialist and communist vision, the nation state was no longer the adequate framework for the organization of social life, as all human beings were considered equal and political institutions no longer seemed required in the projected state of universal harmony, brotherhood and peace. Similar to the guiding principles of postclassical Greek philosophy, they too focused on the human being *in abstracto*, absolved from national affiliations and bonds, and merged into a universal, all-embracing union conceived as one big family of brothers and sisters. Like the Cynics and Epicureans, the socialists and communists called on the individual to abandon any previous commitment, not only to the institutions of the nation state but to all matters of the world including property, possession and power. Like the Cynics and Epicureans, they too called on the human being not to cling and enslave himself to outside, worldly entities, which they considered hindrances to personal autarky, self-sufficiency and subjective autonomy. Undisturbed by politics and worldly concerns, the Cynics and Epicureans in Hellenistic Greece and the socialists and communists in modern Europe took a sensualistic approach and strove for the — greatest possible — satisfaction of natural, physical (or biological) needs. As Hannah Arendt has pointed out, socialism

---

[1] Ferguson, 106, 112.
[2] Ferguson, 129.

and communism aimed for a "unified humanity," in which man was to withdraw from the outside, material world in favor of radical self-sufficiency and introspection, reduced to his basic rational capacity (mental operations) and natural physical existence: Fully focused on enhancing the immediate processes of life, socialism and communism sought to reduce the human being to the antipolitical existence of a living organism, limited essentially to his bodily pleasures, needs and pains.[1] As the Cynics held that man should live like a dog in the street or herd of cattle in the pasture, the radical ideologies of 19th and 20th century Europe strove to transform man into a working animal without adherence to a specifically human world of objects and institutions, i.e., an *animal laborans* which, according to Arendt, would "indeed be only one, at best the highest, of the animal species which populate the earth."[2] The animal laborans as envisaged by the socialists and communists is, in Arendt's words, "ejected from the world in so far as he is imprisoned in the privacy of his own body, caught in the fulfillment of his natural needs ... What Marx had in mind when he spoke of a 'socialised mankind' consists of worldless specimens of the species mankind ..."[3]

In either case, the rise of radical ideology and utopian visions of universal fraternity in a global, post-political community represented reactions — among other things — to a fundamental crisis of the traditional, inherited bodies politic in ancient Greece and modern Europe respectively. In Hellenistic Greece of the fourth and third century B.C., Cynicism and Epicureanism responded to the exhaustion and degradation of the city-state in the age of its eclipse by large monarchical conglomerations through and after Alexander the Great, when the city-states were reduced to second-order status and widely considered to be a too narrow, outdated model of political organization.

In modern Europe, socialism, communism and anarchism all ascended in a situation where the boundaries and institutional structures of the nation state were challenged and undermined by the dynamic forces of capitalist accumulation and imperialist aspiration — i.e., where Europeans felt for the first time that national markets (or frameworks) and the institutions of the nation state were becoming

---

[1] Arendt, *The Human Condition*, London and Chicago 1958, 112.
[2] Arendt, *Human Condition*, 84.
[3] Hannah Arendt, *Human Condition*, 118s.

too small in view of a future, which apparently belonged to larger, postnational conglomerations. In both cases, the decline of confidence in the inherited bodies politic, on which the aspirations and ambitions of the citizens had once been centered, and the shattering experience that the role of the once so ardently venerated (municipal or national) entities was apparently played out, was carried to extremes by the masterminds of radical ideology and utopian vision. (In the eyes of Karl Marx in particular, the nation state — along with private ownership of the means of production — was the greatest hindrance to universal human progress.)

As global trade and the international division of labor were laying waste to the nation states as antiquated models of politico-economic organization, they would finally have to give way to a free association of individuals as members of a unified, socialized mankind. As the city or nation state was in decline and its inherited bodies politic were no longer able to absorb the civic energies, hopes and aspirations, radical ideology and utopian vision took this trend to its extreme conclusion by abandoning any allegiance to the nation or polis, demanding a downright abolition of the state as an institution of compulsion and calling for the complete elimination of any body politic or genuine public sphere.

In particular, the radical apoliticism of postclassical philosophy in ancient Greece and utopian ideology in modern Europe becomes apparent if one takes into consideration the fundamental distinction once made by the ancient Greeks between the oikos as the private sphere and venue of natural and biological functions (the activities required for the preservation of life)[1] and the polis as the public sphere or scene for the matters of the world. In fact, both Cynicism and Epicureanism in ancient Greece and socialism and communism in modern Europe conceived the new, universal community as one big family or globalized oikos, in which a public or political sphere no longer existed and man saw himself reduced to the physical, biological and natural functions of private life, originally located as they were in the secluded sphere of the oikos or house.

No longer embedded in municipal or national political institutions, the individual was to reduce himself to the basic original functions of

---

[1] Cf. Arendt, *Human Condition*, 30: "The distinctive trait of the household sphere was that in it men lived together because they were driven by their wants and needs."

the oikos, i.e., revert back to his bodily needs and physical functions and become transformed into a bare living being and biological creature. (In Hellenistic Greece, the degradation of the original public or political sphere was reflected most strikingly in the Cynics' ostentatious display of natural biological functions like sexuality or urination in the public space, which had always been considered as the most private elements of human life, designated for public invisibility, in classical Greek political thought.)

In the case of ancient Cynicism, as in the case of modern communism, man's diminution to the basic natural functions originally located in the oikos or house is a reflection of radical worldlessness, where man is no longer considered to be a zoon politicon or constructor of outside reality, i.e., no longer needs to concern himself with the matters of the world but seeks reduction to an animalistic minimum and confines himself to the satisfaction of natural needs and biological (animalistic) drives.

On the other hand, it was by no means accidental that the forces of radical ideology and utopian vision have met with consistently fierce resistance in ancient Rome as well as in modern America. In the case of ancient Rome, Cato the Elder insisted on the immediate dismissal of an embassy of Greek philosophers, led by Carneades the Skeptic in 155 B.C., who had questioned the authority of the Roman state and criticized the practices of Roman politics as a breach of human equality, brotherhood and universal law.

For Roman politicians of the second century B.C., it was still good custom — despite the rising influence of Greek philosophical thought — to dissociate oneself at least publicly from Greek universalistic and cosmopolitan ideas (humanitas), reject Epicurean and Cynic radicalism and emphasize one's lasting commitment to the original, national spirit of Rome.

In the United States, the "European" ideas of socialism, communism and anarchism were fiercely suppressed during the "Red Scare" after World War I and then, even more prominently, during the McCarthy era after World War II. Like Stoic and Epicurean philosophers who were repeatedly expelled from Rome in the second century B.C. on the grounds of threatening allegiance to the Roman spirit and state, adherents of the radical left were fiercely suppressed after World War I when the U.S. authorities preventively deported thousands of communists and anarchists to Russia. In an attempt to hunt down Soviet spies and prevent the (allegedly) impending Communist infiltration of key industries and government institutions, thousands of teachers, union leaders, journalists, screenwriters, movie actors, producers and radio commentators were blacklisted since the late 1940s or required to appear before the House Committee on Un-American Activities (HUAC), orchestrated by Senator Joseph McCarthy in the 1950s.

During the second century B.C., the Roman authorities still attempted to protect national loyalty and allegiance from imminent infiltration by Greek skepticism and cosmopolitan ideas by refusing to tolerate the presence of radical Greek philosophers within the confines of the city. In a similar way, members of the European communist parties were consistently banned from entering and traveling to the United States after World War II.

Again, the sustained rejection of Epicureanism, Stoicism and Cynicism in ancient Rome and of anarchism, socialism and communism in the United States has much to do with the special reverence paid by the Romans and Americans for their constitutional frameworks and fabrics, for which it is impossible to find a match in any other nation or political entity of their respective ages and times.

Taking into consideration that radical ideology and utopian vision in ancient Greece and modern Europe represented, among other things, an extreme response to the fundamental crisis or collapse of the inherited bodies politic, turning their backs on the patrimonial set of political institutions and calling for a general withdrawal from politics to private life (the immediate needs and concerns of the self), it is only logical that they were (or are) unable to prevail in ancient Rome or modern America for as long as the Romans and Americans remain(ed) so ardently loyal to their ancestral constitutional frameworks and tied to the inherited institutions of their respective bodies politic. Accordingly, radical ideology did not begin to assert itself in Rome until the grave and finally lethal crisis of the republic in the first century B.C., when identification with the republican institutions decreased and confidence in the lastingness of the constitution began to falter.

Way into the first century B.C., Greek philosophy in general did not have a good reputation in Rome (even for Cicero, his philosophical activities "were always secondary to his political interests and ambitions, and were pursued only ... in periods of enforced withdrawal from the political center-stage"[1]), and Stoicism did not prevail as the predominant school of thought in Rome until the republican institutions eventually collapsed and the focus of life began shifting away from political activity and care for the common good to inner freedom, personal self-sufficiency and subjective concerns. Only in those days, when the citizens no longer believed in their collective capacity of shaping public affairs, which had passed into the hands of a few extremely wealthy and powerful individuals, did the Romans withdraw from civic virtue in favor of the occupation with one's own personal self and subjective needs.

In fact, it was not until the first century B.C. either, i.e., during the collapse of the republican institutions and the gradual establishment of the empire, that Cynicism and Epicureanism firmly established themselves in Rome. Lucretius, who rose to prominence at around 60 B.C., and Virgil (70 B.C.–19 B.C.) were the first major Roman poets committed to the ideas of Epicurus, and Horace (65 B.C–8 A.D.) even referred to himself explicitly (in a letter to Tibullus) as a "pig from the herd of Epicurus."[2]

Only in the first century A.D. did the figure of the cynic appear in the streets of Rome, who begged, preached and slept in the open air, proudly doing without a family or home and turning his back on politics and possession. Disregarding the outside world and living the lives of migrant preachers, the cynics occupied themselves entirely with mental concerns, physical needs and the continuous observation of their own personal souls. Only from the fundamental crisis and inner corruption of the republic in the first century B.C. onwards did political activity and civic action come to be regarded as something vulgar, as people no longer sought to serve the institutions of the state and concern themselves with public (or worldly) affairs.

Not until the crisis and downfall of the republic and in the age of the humanitarian emperors, when the republic and its institutions had already receded into history, did the Roman elites regard themselves as citizens of the world and members of a universal cosmopolitan community along Greek philosophical lines — guided by a ruler whose most important task it was to promote peace and brotherhood

---

[1] David Stockton, *Cicero. A Political Biography*, Oxford 1971, VII.
[2] Horace, *Epistles*, I, IV, 16.

among his peoples, govern in a spirit of clemency, practice universal philanthropy towards all members of mankind *(salus generis humani)* and continuously scrutinize his own personal self. Declining all former commitment and allegiance to the city, the national spirit and the laws of Rome, Stoicism and Cynicism of the post-republican age (as epitomized in Seneca and Epictetus) taught obedience to the universal nature of man, as the focus of life shifted from politics to self-perfection, self-development and the inner review of human conscience. Only now was freedom re-defined as inner autonomy, personal self-sufficiency and subjective peace of mind, and no longer considered as a basically political category.

Given the determination of radical ideology to disregard the political sphere and matters of the outside world in favor of the human being's personal (subjective) autonomy, immediate physical needs and mental concerns, such ideas could only prosper at a time when the body politic and constitutional framework of the nation were fundamentally questioned or in a virtual state of collapse, and civic political action was no longer a promising and desirable prospect.

Only once the "love of the world" had vanished, which had used to be so characteristic of the original, national spirit of Rome (i.e., when the once so strong respect for the constitutional system gave way to political disillusionment, and Roman politics dissociated itself from national interest and national institutions), could the forces of radical ideology and utopian vision finally emerge victorious.

Once the citizens saw themselves stripped of the opportunity to take civic action and shape the world by political means, the resigning, apolitical attitudes of postclassical Greek philosophy (where man was declared unable to control the outside entities and realities, which he therefore had to accept with the greatest possible equanimity) were eventually able to prevail. On the same supposition, however, there is much to suggest that any sustained success of cosmopolitan, socialist or communist thought seems unlikely in the United States for as long as Americans retain confidence in the power and authority of their constitution and remain convinced that their framework of political institutions is still vigorous, up for the challenges of the future, and hence deserves persistent loyalty, allegiance and commitment. (As we shall see towards the end of the book, however, things look different when it comes to the increasing intellectual relevance not of classical socialism and communism, but of a softer, cultural version of Marxism promoting the deconstruction of nation, race and gender in favor of a cosmopolitan society of radically free, disconnected and solipsistic individuals.)

11. Ancestral Lands, Mobility and Depopulation

The general observation that many socio-political, cultural and intellectual phenomena characteristic of the Hellenistic age in ancient Greece recurred in Rome during or after the collapse of the republican institutions in the first century B.C. does not only hold true, however, for the universalistic, cosmopolitan ideas of Cynic and Stoic philosophical thought. For instance, it was by no means accidental that depopulation and declining birthrates especially among the former political and social elites became a serious problem for Rome only after the crisis and downfall of the republican system.

By contrast, Hellenistic Greece had already suffered from this predicament two hundred years before, when the historian Polybius called depopulation the doom of Greece and lamented in the second century B.C.: "In our time, the whole of Greece has suffered from low birthrates and a general decrease in the population, as a result of which the cities have become deserted and the land has ceased to yield fruit although we have not been hit by any great war or major epidemic in recent time."[1]

In many famous cities of ancient Greece, entire urban quarters were deserted, while grains grew in the amphitheaters and livestock grazed in the former popular assembly places. As a consequence, already King Philip V of Macedon furthered immigration from Thrace and other fringe regions of the Hellenistic world, but he also took a number of measures

---

[1] Polybius, *The Histories*, Book XXXVI, Section V.

to raise birthrate levels including the obligation for every male and female member of an upper class family to have and raise children.

Obviously, similar developments are observable today in many regions of Europe including the Ruhr Valley, East Germany, Italy, Spain and large parts of Eastern Europe, where birthrates have declined dramatically and depopulation has turned into a serious problem. Throughout the regions most affected by population shrinking, schools are closed, villages abandoned and public transport facilities shut down. At the same time, rows of houses or entire urban quarters are knocked down to halt dilapidation and prevent a painful slump in local house prices.

In Germany for instance, the number of births has halved from 1.3 million a year in 1960 to 650,000 in 2009 despite high birthrate levels among the steadily rising immigrant population. In other countries like Poland, Italy or Spain, the situation looks even worse, as fertility rates remain well below the rate of reproduction.[1] According to projections by the demographic research agency Eurostat, the German population alone would decrease from 82 to 32 million by 2100, while Italy would be down from 57 to 15 million and Spain reduced from 39 to 12 million if present trends continue.

For several years already, European politicians have tried to counter the increased levels of childlessness especially among high-income earners by offering financial incentives like parental benefits, family credits and other procreation-supporting contributions in combination with publicly funded kindergartens and children's day care centers. At the same time, immigration from the bordering nations of Europe is widely considered the only way of sustaining the current levels of population and maintaining the established standards of social security and wealth.

Like the cities of postclassical Greece which loosened the once strict distinction between citizens and strangers and started awarding citizenship — including the right to acquire landed property — to foreigners (who played an increasingly prominent role, e.g., in the economy of Athens, as bankers, shipbuilders and grain importers), the nations of postwar Europe are adopting policies of extensive immigration and naturalization of foreigners so as to fill the land and

---

[1] Cf. Laqueur, 190s.

compensate for the massive decrease in natality among the original indigenous population.

In the case of ancient Greece, especially the large Hellenistic cities had multiethnic and multireligious populations, as the merging of different ethnic groups had been a general policy of the Hellenistic rulers ever since Alexander the Great. (Already at the mass wedding arranged by Alexander at Susa in 324 B.C., 90 of his confidants had married the daughters of Persian greats, and similar policies were later pursued as well by the Seleucid and Ptolemaic kings of Syria and Egypt respectively. This openness to foreigners or other ethnic groups stood in striking contrast with the original nature of the classical city states as closed communities, where only very few foreigners had been allowed to become citizens, intermarriage with outsiders had been discouraged, and the right to own land had been limited to natives.)

In Europe, it is estimated that major cities including Birmingham, Amsterdam, Brussels, Cologne and Marseille will no longer have a native population majority already within three to four decades, taking into account that 55–75% of present-day school children have immigration backgrounds. Considering the high fertility among immigrants, ethnic Europeans are expected to form a minority from the end of the 21st century onwards.[1] Although state-subsidized paid parental leave, government-funded nursery centers and public kindergartens are very rare in the United States, where the raising of one's children is still considered to be essentially a private matter, childbirth rates in America are in fact significantly higher than in Europe and suffice to sustain the current level of population. (According to figures quoted by Robert Kagan, the average age in the United States will rise from 35.5 to 36.2 by 2050, while the Europeans are currently 37.7 and predicted to reach 52.7 years on average in 2050.[2])

---

[1] Laqueur, 193s. According to UN projections, the indigenous population of Europe will drop to 59 million by 2300, with many European nations down to 5% or, in the case of Italy and Russia, even 1% of their current population levels (Laqueur, 197). At the same time, a UN report published under the title of "Replacement Migration" projects that 700 million immigrants will be needed for the period from 1995 to 2050 to maintain the European economies, that France, Germany, Belgium, the Netherlands, Scandinavia and the UK will cease having native population majorities in the second half of this century and that Europe will turn predominantly Islamic by 2100 (Laqueur, 198).

[2] Kagan, 55.

At least in major sections of American society, one still finds a basically more positive attitude towards having children, which are not so much considered a disturbance, a career obstacle and a burdensome threat to self-realization as in many parts of Europe. Whereas the institution of the family and family values are still highly esteemed in the United States, their standing has declined dramatically in many parts of Europe, where people have become increasingly unwilling to sacrifice immediate personal interests for the sake of pregnancy, parental obligation and family life. In Germany for instance, the National Institute of Population Research tried to foster understanding for the indigenous population's soaring reluctance to have children by presenting a calculation, according to which every person having a child in Germany is poised to lose a total spendable income of EUR 266,000 due to the costs entailed in rearing a child.[1]

Whereas the *old worlds* of Greece and Europe respectively suffer(ed) from childlessness and depopulation, birthrates in the United States and — for long periods of time — in ancient Rome have remained essentially sufficient to maintain the respective levels of population.[2] Considering the fundamental differences distinguishing the "old" worlds of Europe and Greece and the "new," ascending powers of America and Rome in terms of mental constitution and socio-political values, there is much to suggest that the diverging rates of reproduction do trace back, after all, to the differing degrees of confidence in the nation, loyalty to the national bodies politic (or constitutional frameworks) and allegiance to the inherited ancestral lands.

In fact, the ancient Romans and modern Americans were (or are) not only committed to their constitutions and national bodies politic but also to their ancestral land and soil, in a way which was (or is) no longer to be found in Hellenistic Greece or postclassical Europe. For long periods of time, the Romans adhered to the principle of the *militia continuata* with peasant-citizen soldiers defending the land which they cultivated and tilled, driven by an ardent commitment to the country, family, fields and state. For the early Romans, farmland work with calloused hands was not considered a shameful and despicable occupation as in many sections of the more "progressive" Hellenistic

---

[1] Laqueur, 284.
[2] Madden, 139.

east; it was perceived explicitly as a badge of honor.[1] Early Roman culture was essentially agrarian, as the Roman values emanated from a farming context, Roman religion was centered on the family farm and Romans venerated the spirit of the ancestral soil.[2] In a manual on agriculture, Cato the Elder claimed that it was always "from the ranks of the farmers that the bravest men and sturdiest soldiers come."[3]

The very epitome of the Roman farmer-patriot and citizen-soldier was Lucius Quinctius Cincinnatus, who readily returned to his plough after saving the republic — threatened by an assault from neighboring tribes — as a 16 days' dictator in 458 B.C. While Romans of that period still saw themselves essentially as farmers, tied and confined to their ancestral homeland and soil, the Hellenistic Greeks looked down on the alleged vulgarity and "boorishness" of the Roman generals, whom they regarded as the offspring of poorly educated Italian peasants.[4] Despite seeing the Hellenistic kingdoms collapse like houses of cards before the Roman legions and reduced to political insignificance or second order status by the Romans, most Hellenistic Greeks still fancied themselves culturally and intellectually superior — as the inventors of philosophy and science — to the herdsmen, bumpkins and boors from the allegedly semi-barbaric West.[5]

Like Roman values two thousand years ago, however, the basic values of America also emanate from the land and soil with a strong devotion to piety, patriotism, perseverance and hard, field-tilling work.[6] The national and commercial culture of the United States is steeped in a farming and frontier tradition, as presidents and presidential candidates are eager to present themselves as ranchers like Bush, cowboys like Reagan or peanut farmers like Carter.

In a manner structurally similar to that of Cato the Elder, Thomas Jefferson claimed that the "cultivators of the land are the most valuable citizens. They are the most vigorous, the most independent, the most virtuous, and they are tied to their country and wedded to its liberty and interests by the most lasting bonds."[7] Yet while many Americans

---

[1] Madden, 42.
[2] Madden, 14.
[3] As quoted in Madden, 39.
[4] Madden, 153ss.
[5] Madden, 78 / 153ss.
[6] Madden, 14.
[7] As quoted in George Packer, *The Unwinding. An Inner History of the New America*, New York 2013, 77s.

today still share Jefferson's view, the farmer/countryman has come to be regarded as a ridiculous, despicable figure in postwar Europe as he was in Hellenistic Greece. Most Europeans fancy themselves more clever, advanced and civilized than the allegedly primitive (or backward) population of mainland USA, whom they tend to associate with superficiality, poor education and a grave lack of culture. When supposedly clever Europeans mock elections in heartland America, i.e., the rural areas and small towns of the South and Midwest, as being decided by poorly educated farmers and country bumpkins living on the dark side of the moon, their attitudes illustrate how strikingly similar the disparaging assessment of modern Americans by the Europeans is to the sustained disdain once shown for the ancient Romans by the Hellenistic Greeks.

In the final analysis, there is much to indicate that childbirth rates and procreation levels have something to do, among other things, with the level of determination to pass on the worshipped land and soil to a next generation and perpetuate the venerated institutions of the body politic. Conversely, the inclination to have children seems to recede once people become less committed to their nation and land and cease believing in the durability and lasting strength of their national bodies politic. In a certain way, high levels of childlessness result from a loss of love for the world, of identification with the nation and belief in the vigor and authority of the national political frameworks and constitutions.

In Hellenistic Greece and postwar Europe, however, people came (or have come) to focus essentially on the needs of the self and withdraw from public affairs in favor of inner perception and personal experience, no longer aspiring to perpetuate the institutional framework of the polis or nation state and less determined to pass on the inherited lands to a next generation. Clearly, one was less committed to the country, nation and ancestral lands in postclassical Greece, where the educated classes tended to hold cosmopolitan views and no longer saw themselves as members of a particular city or nation state but basically as individuals, human beings *in abstracto* and citizens of the world — committed to their own personal aspirations and subjective concerns rather than to the land or the institutions of the state.

Especially in the large cities of the Hellenistic world, the figure of the farmer met with open contempt and explicit disdain. Whereas Romans of the same period still considered themselves essentially as farmers, proud of their ancestral homeland and soil, the farmer and countryman had long been a subject of mockery and contempt in Hellenistic theater, sculpture and art. In addition, the military no longer consisted of small farmers and peasant proprietors determined to defend their polis and their own small piece of land, as was the case in the classical age, but of mercenaries, foreigners and professional career troops.[1]

In present-day Europe, the situation is very similar in principle as people have embraced postnational views and ceased believing that their traditional, national bodies politic still have the capacity of mastering the challenges of the future. In fact, many Europeans hold that, sooner or later, their national institutions should be replaced with larger entities and postnational conglomerations like the European Union or even the United Nations.

At the same time, the farmer and countryman has become a despicable figure as well in postwar Europe, much in contrast to his lasting recognition and prestige in the United States. In both cases, as a result, there is much to suggest that the rising levels of childlessness and increasing depopulation are linked with a decline in commitment to the land, a loss of national ambition and a lack of confidence in the vigor and authority of the constitutional (municipal or national) frameworks. No longer aspiring to perpetuate their bodies politic and hand their ancestral soil down to generations of descendants, both the Hellenistic Greeks and postwar Europeans saw (or see) less need to have children.

The reasons habitually given by many Europeans for not having children — i.e., the loss of personal independence, career prospects and individual quality of life — clearly indicate that they view themselves primarily as individuals, focusing on subjective needs and concerns (personal advancement and individual self-realization), and no longer as members of a nation, people and ancestral line deserving to be continued into the distant future by generations of children and grandchildren.

---

[1] Mossé, 171.

No longer believing that they still have historical missions to fulfill and considering their historical energies to be used up, postclassical (i.e., essentially individualistic) Greeks and Europeans no longer see a need to preserve and perpetuate their territorial, ethnic or cultural identities and communities. As a consequence, they tend to refrain from having children, resort to multiethnic societal concepts and seek compensation for the shrinking levels of the indigenous population through large-scale immigration, as they rely on immigrants to secure economic prosperity and fill the (prospectively) desolated lands. Viewing themselves as human beings and members of mankind, the Hellenistic Greeks and present-day Europeans shy away from the endeavors of defending their cultures, nations, heritage and traditions.

Against this backdrop, the decline of procreation levels in Hellenistic Greece and postwar Europe respectively is not simply, as Spengler held, a symptom of a high culture's bio-societal exhaustion and old age; rather it stands in causal connection with a loss of belief in the lasting capacity of the national political institutions (or bodies politic) and a decrease in commitment to the inherited ancestral homeland and soil. (We shall see, against this backdrop, whether the United States will indeed someday have to incorporate an ailing Europe, which fails to cope with the challenges of its multi-ethnic societies and cultures or threatens to succumb to radical Islam, into its political order and domain — as Rome once did after the Greeks, having abandoned their sense of national identity and togetherness, had made themselves available to alien, non-Greek causes in the Mithridatic Wars.)

In Rome itself, childlessness and depopulation did not become a serious problem until the late first century B.C., when we begin to see extremely low reproduction rates, and the number of divorces, unmarried people and childless marriages surged especially among the former political elites of the disempowered Roman republic. (As we saw above, this was also the time when the Cynic idea of life without a wife, a family and a home managed to firmly establish itself within the city of Rome.) In 18 B.C. and 9 B.C. respectively, the Emperor Augustus hence enacted his famous marriage and morality legislation (*lex de maritandis ordinibus*) in a desperate attempt to encourage the conclusion of marriages and bolster reproduction through a combination of incentive and compulsion. Under the new imperial law, men aged 25 to 60 and women aged 20 to 50 were compelled to marry including the obligation to remarry in case of the spouse's death. While those having three or more children were favored in terms of taxation and promotion in the imperial administration, the inheritance rights of unmarried or childless subjects was restricted. In the end, however, it proved impossible to halt the decline of the population despite the imperial marriage legislation and the increased settlement of barbarian peoples and soldiers on Roman soil, through which Augustus and his imperial successors tried to fill the desolated lands. With the disempowerment and eventual liquidation of the republic, the patrician families and the traditional (agrarian and artisanal) plebs were stripped of their original mission to preserve the constitution, perpetuate the body politic and serve as supporting pillars of the Roman state. After the lingering crisis and final collapse of the republican institutions, it was therefore only logical that Romans focused more, since the first century B.C., on the needs and concerns of the self rather than on public, political and national affairs. Indeed, these were times — as we shall see in greater detail in Chapter 13 — when traditional ties to the national interest and soil were loosened on a general scale as a consequence of social, constitutional and geopolitical change: in social terms, many small peasants and freehold farmers were expelled from their ancestral lands and filled the swelling ranks of the urban proletariat in the city of Rome, which became completely disconnected from the former spirit of the lands and fields. In constitutional terms, political activity and responsibility became a matter no longer of the people or even the senatorial elite but rather of very few immensely rich individuals and, finally, the emperor and his administration.

Geopolitically, Roman policies more and more dissociated themselves as well from national interest and national territory, as they turned towards expansion and the conquest, suppression and exploitation of foreign, ever more distant nations. In a time, however, when the former political elites and supporting social pillars of the Roman state were deprived of their original task to sustain the institutions of the republic, hand down their land to sons and grandsons, and secure the future of the nation — i.e., when commitment to the ancestral land and soil was replaced with cosmopolitan, Stoical or Cynicist views, and the slogan of *"ubi bene, ibi patria*" came into fashion — it was almost inevitable that the need for reproduction dwindled and the incentive for procreation decreased, as had been the case two centuries before in the Hellenistic period of ancient Greece.

Besides, the question of allegiance to the nation and commitment to the inherited ancestral also relates intrinsically to the subject and respective level of geographical mobility. For long periods of time, a strong distinction was in place between the essentially conservative, earthbound spirit of the Romans and the more "progressive" attitudes of the Hellenistic world, where wide sections of the population had become mobile and begun detaching themselves from traditional confinement to the individual city-state.

On the trading routes and cobbled roads of the Hellenistic world, entire groups of professionals were on their way from mainland Greece to the new centers of power in North Africa and Minor Asia: mercenaries from the cities of heartland Greece who went east in search of employment by one of the Hellenistic monarchs; athletes seeking fame and rewards at one of the regional or supra-regional competitions; poets and performing artists hoping to be contracted as "artists of Dionysus" for a festival or royal court, and other occupational groups like doctors, sculptors, traders, philosophers, musicians, architects, engineers or master-builders.[1]

At the same time, tourists visited the monuments, sanctuaries and miracles of nature of the Hellenistic lands including Ephesus, Knidos, Kos, Rhodes, Troy, the thermal springs of Hierapolis or the sinkholes of Cennet and Cehennem. Often, they relied on the recommendations given by travel guides, the most famous of which included the one by Herakleides Kritikos, who described the sights of ancient Greece in his literarily ambitious treatise *On the Cities of Greece*, assumed to have been published in 309 B.C.[2] In the third century B.C., Diodoros the Perieget described the settlements, monuments and sights of Attica, and Agatharchides merged scientific curiosity with touristic interest in a highly popular guide to the Red Sea region.

While Greek tourists and professionals assiduously traveled the Hellenistic world, Romans of the same period still saw themselves essentially as farmers and peasants, bound to their inherent homeland

---

[1] On mobility in Hellenistic Greece, cf. Walbank, 68ss.
[2] Cf. François Chamoux, *Hellenistic Civilisation*, Oxford 2003, 315ss., Walbank, 211ss., André 109.

and tied to their ancestral soil. A structurally similar situation is observable today within the West, as Europeans tend to travel extensively more than the Americans and are astonished to learn that only about 20 percent of all U.S. citizens actually hold a passport.

Similar to the ancient Romans' confinement to their own inherited land and rootedness in their own ancestral soil, many Americans take pride in never having traveled to a foreign country and being more or less ignorant about the rest of the world. In both cases, we are faced with conflicting mental constitutions and cultural patterns between a civilization, which has come out of touch with its inherited lands and ceased believing in the vigor and capacity of the city or nation on the one hand (i.e., postclassical Greece and Europe respectively) and ascending superpowers on the other, whose people have remained intensely committed to their constitutional frameworks and firmly tied to their ancestral homeland and soil.

In spite of all the haughtiness and contempt shown for the Romans by the ancient Greeks, however, clear-sighted Greek philosophers, scholars and rhetoricians of the first and second century B.C. knew very well that, if they were to play a relevant role in politics and current affairs, they had to establish themselves in Rome or become part of the entourage of an influential Roman senator, diplomat or army commander.

In a similar manner, modern scientists in Europe are well aware — despite a general haughtiness among many Europeans concerning the Americans' alleged lack of culture, shallowness and poor education — that working at a U.S. university or research institution is by far the most promising way to achieve international excellence or rise to a worldwide reputation.

Politically, any prudent politician within the ruling elites of postclassical Greece and Europe respectively understood (or understands) very well that, to prosper, survive and live in peace, the Greeks and Europeans need(ed) to remain on good terms with the superpower, accept their basically subordinate role and not shrink back if necessary from showing a certain degree of unquestioned obedience and self-humiliation.

By contrast, there has been nothing to await for any power or political undertaking in ancient Greece and modern Europe, which dared to defy the superpower, except for subjection and defeat by the vastly superior war machine, economic potential and diplomatic resources of the Romans and Americans respectively — be it the Germans in World War II, the Russians in the Cold War, the Serbians in the 1990s, or be it Perseus III, the last king of the Macedonians, the Greek city states supporting the anti-Roman campaign of Mithridates VI in the early first century B.C. or the Seleucid king Antiochus IV, around whom a Roman envoy once drew a line in the sand and told him not to pass outside the circle before bowing unconditionally to the claims and demands of Rome.

12. RELUCTANT HEGEMONS

As has often been observed, both the ancient Romans and the modern Americans did not actively seek the ascension to global hegemony, the extension of their reach beyond the own borders, direct governmental control over other nations or the systematic establishment of imperial rule. Instead, they both expanded very slowly, cautiously and in a spirit of reluctance, as the road to hegemony was not paved with an innate expansionary impulse to rule and dominate the world but rather with defensive motivations, security interests and the need to prevent the rise of dangerous rivals potentially threatening the respective *spheres of influence.*[1]

In fact, the Romans were very hesitant to enter the First and Second Punic Wars, finally seeing no choice but to protect their allies and prevent Carthaginian control over Southern Italy and Spain respectively, which would have posed an immediate threat to the city's fundamental security interests. Prior to the Second Punic War, the Romans patiently tolerated Carthage's aggressive policy in Spain, did not respond to Saguntum's (their Spanish ally's) call for aid and only declared war on the Carthaginians after Hannibal had crossed the river Ebro and thus explicitly breached the Roman-Carthaginian treaty. In 219 B.C., they showed extensive patience in trying to solve the dispute on piracy with the Illyrians by peaceful means and only took up arms after their envoys and negotiators had been murdered by order of the Illyrian king. In 200 B.C., the Romans intervened militarily

---

[1] Madden, 77.

for the first time in Greece after King Philip V of Macedon had attacked Pergamum and Athens, and hence threatened to dominate the Aegean Sea and turn into a dangerous threat to Rome's maritime security concerns. A few years later, it was the Seleucid king Antiochus the Great who invaded Rome's new sphere of influence in Greece, but he saw his army crushed by the Roman troops. He finally had to renounce his claims to Greece and Asia Minor, surrender his warships and pay the gargantuan war indemnity of 15,000 talents of silver.[1]

In modern times, the United States was equally hesitant to enter World War I and World War II, as the American public supported neutrality, and Wilson and Roosevelt were highly popular because they "kept us out of the war." In fact, not even the prospect of a German-dominated Europe or a "totalitarian world" with a Nazi Empire over Europe and a Japanese Empire over Asia managed to convince the American electorate that entering the war had become inevitable. At the end of the day, it took Germany's unlimited submarine warfare in 1917 (in addition to secret offers by German agents to aid Mexican revolutionaries trying to regain lost territories in Texas, New Mexico and Arizona) and the Japanese attack on Pearl Harbor, combined with Hitler's declaration of war in 1941, to make America enter World War I and World War II respectively.

Over long periods of the time, the Romans and Americans rarely started a major war themselves; instead, they were either attacked by enemies or talked into the war by allies who called the Romans and Americans to their aid. In 264 and 218 B.C. respectively, the Romans entered the First and Second Punic Wars on request from their allies in Southern Italy (the Mamertines) and Spain (Saguntum). In the second century B.C., embassies and delegations from the cities and states of Greece persistently requested Roman aid against rivaling Greek powers, municipalities and states.

Steadily Greek leaders, kings or pretenders sent missions to Rome seeking support of their interests and asking for military suppression of their foes, anxiously longing for the installation of a Roman savior and protector. In 201 B.C., for instance, Rhodes and Pergamum asked Rome for military support against the expansionist policies pursued by King Philip V of Macedon in the years leading up to the Second Macedonian War (200–197 B.C.). Roman intervention was also

---

[1] Pearson, 111s.

requested in 194 B.C., when Sparta, the Aitolians, and Antiochus III of Syria had joined forces to seek expansion at the expense of the minor powers and city-states of mainland Greece.

In modern history, the United States did not intervene into the affairs of Europe until persuaded by Britain and France to enter World War I in 1917 and by Churchill to join World War II in 1941. In both cases, the action was billed as coming to Europe's rescue in the face of a German quest for hegemony.

After World War II, military interventions by the United States and the establishment of military bases in Europe, the Pacific and East Asia were sparked, at least initially, by fear of the Soviet Union and China, i.e., the need to contain the expansionist objectives and aspirations of communism. During the course of the cold war, the U.S. intervened in various countries, built military bases and committed itself more intensively to Europe through the establishment of NATO and the permanent deployment of American troops on Western European soil, all on the basis of a fear of Soviet influence and the need to protect its allies in the face of potential communist aggression.

As a matter of course, security interests and defensive motivations do not account for the entire story of Roman and American expansion and ascension to hegemony. Clearly, expansion was also driven by other momenta such as the need for young Roman aristocrats to acquire military fame in the context of foreign campaigns and the interest in exploiting the material resources of a new province — or by the urge to open foreign markets to U.S. surplus production, investment and trade, and to secure the supply of cheap natural resources.

Nevertheless, Peter Bender has a point in claiming that "Rome and America both expanded to achieve security. Like concentric circles, each circle in need of security demanded the occupation of the next larger circle. The Romans made their way around the Mediterranean, driven from one challenge to their security to the next. The struggles against Hitler, Stalin, Mao and Japan brought the Americans to Europe and East Asia. The Americans soon wound up all over the globe, driven from one attempt at containment to the next."[1]

Eventually, the need to defend and protect first Roman and U.S. soil, and then the spheres of influence established as buffer zones in

[1] Peter Bender, "The New Rome," in: Andrew C. Bacevich (ed.), *The Imperial Tense. Problems and Prospects of American Empire*, Chicago 2003, 81-92, 82.

search of enhanced security and enemy containment, inescapably gave rise to policies of progressive expansion. Having fought existential enemies and countered existential threats (in the Punic Wars, the two World Wars and the Cold War respectively), both the Romans and the Americans finally found themselves having accrued unprecedented levels of potency and power. Almost inadvertently, the United States found itself — after 1945 — in control of a majority of the world's economic resources, along with overwhelming military strength, superior arms technology, a network of military bases stretching across four continents, and sustained cultural, economic and financial predominance .

Anxious to avoid entanglement and formal commitment abroad, however, the ascending superpowers have tended to refrain from the establishment of direct (governmental) control over the "old" worlds of Greece and Europe. For long periods of time, both the Romans and the Americans have been explicitly reluctant to occupy, conquer and annex, preferring instead to withdraw their victorious troops from Greece and Europe after having brought provisional stability and preliminary peace. Often, it has been claimed that the hegemonic practices of the Romans and the Americans were essentially and categorically different, as America does not conquer and acquire territories, establish provinces or exercise forms of direct (governmental) rule over other countries and nations. Yet throughout most of Rome's republican period, the Romans' way of handling things was not through subjugation, territorial acquisition, foreign conquest and centralized sovereign rule. (This indicates once again that the standard of reference for present-day America is not the Roman Empire, and not even the days of Cicero, Caesar, the civil wars and the proscriptions, but rather, as we shall see further below, the early days of Rome's late republican period.)

In particular, this became evident in 196 B.C., when the Roman general Titus Quinctius Flaminius proclaimed universal freedom for the states of Greece at the Isthmian Games in Corinth and announced the withdrawal of all Roman troops. Refusing to re-arrange the political geography of Greece, Flaminius told the astonished representatives from across the Hellenistic world that, despite its sweeping military victory over the major powers of Greece, Rome would leave the Greeks free, without Roman garrisons or tributary obligations, and subject only to their own governments and laws. In structural terms, this corresponds to the year 1919, when the United States pulled out of Europe and resumed a traditional, isolationist policy after having brought preliminary peace and a shaky institutional order to Europe through its crucial intervention into World War I and its initiation of the League of Nations.

Rather than pursuing policies of systematic imperialist expansion, both superpowers confined themselves, for long periods of time, to hegemonic systems of informal control and indirect command, in which defeated enemies were turned into (dependent) allies, whom the Romans and Americans helped rebuild after the infliction of crushing military defeat.[1] In particular, both superpowers used their financial and economic superiority to secure the allegiance of allies and second-tier powers in Greece and Europe respectively through a combination of economic pressure and incentive.

Throughout the second century B.C., the Romans tried to ensure the loyalty of Greece by redirecting the flows of trade and granting commercial privileges, for instance, to the ports of Athens (Delos) and Rhodes. Rather than annexing other countries and exercising direct governmental control, they strove to create a network of client kingdoms and vassal nations, with whom coalitions could be formed as required on a case-by-case basis.

In modern times, the United States secured the loyalty of Western Europe not only through military might but mainly through financial assistance and economic redevelopment aid as provided under the Dawes and Young Plan after World War I and the Marshall Plan after World War II, which proved to be a very effective instrument for turning Western Europe into an economically prosperous and politically reliable bulwark, ready to accept U.S. supremacy and immune from communist persuasion and seduction. In addition, the role of the U.S. dollar as the world's reserve currency and America's dominance of the global market through international financial organizations like the IMF, the World Bank and the WTO have been employed to exercise U.S. control over its own dependent allies, vassal nations and client states.[2]

---

[1] Madden, 11.

[2] According to David Marquand, the global market is essentially an American construct, underpinned by U.S. military power and shaped by American financial interests (David Marquand, "Playground Bully," in: Bacevich (ed.), 111-118, 113).

By and large, informal control, trade agreements, the promotion of American culture and the American way of life, the vast network of military bases (airfields, naval bases and army garrisons) and the provision of support to pro-American, pro-business governments around the world are making dispensable, at least for the time being, any immediate formal annexation and forms of direct governmental control.

Under systems of informal rule and indirect control, both the Romans and the Americans created a structure of alliances wherein military and foreign policy was (or is) largely determined by the superpower, while the allies were (or are) allowed to govern their own domestic affairs in return for geopolitical subordination, economic allegiance and occasional military support. (At the same time, the Romans and Americans carefully saw or see to it that their allies and client nations remain loyal through informal networks of political and commercial interest and the exertion of influence by means of pro-Roman or pro-American political, intellectual or journalistic lobbyists, elites and representatives of interest trained to serve Roman or American purposes within the respective vassal nations.)

Like Rome established a network of allies in the Hellenistic east and acted as a guarantor of Greek freedom against the looming Macedonian threat, the United States has protected the freedom of Western Europe against an impending Soviet assault. For as long as it proved possible, however, the Romans avoided the assumption of direct administrative responsibility for the Hellenistic cities and states. In fact, they were as anxious to avoid becoming entangled in the inner conflicts and divisions of Greece as America was eager to avoid becoming entangled in the conflicts and quarrels of Europe prior to 1945.

At the end of the day, it was not the initiative of modern America or ancient Rome but the enduring inability of the Greeks and Europeans to manage their own affairs, provide lasting (political and economic) stability and find peaceful solutions to their conflicts which eventually caused, and allowed, the superpowers to intervene and exercise tighter forms of control over the "old," Greek and European worlds. Since the second century B.C., the Greeks themselves incessantly approached the Romans, requesting them to assume responsibility for the affairs of Greece and no longer confine themselves to mere diplomatic conferences and temporary cooperation. Yet even after several of the Hellenistic rulers had virtually willed their kingdoms to Rome — such as Ptolemy Apion of Cyrene, in 96 B.C., Attalus III of Pergamum in 133 B.C. and Ptolemy Alexander I of Egypt in 88 B.C. — the Romans remained reluctant to accept the bequests and refused to answer the plea for annexation.[1]

Only in the face of sustained instability and conflict among the cities, kingdoms and states of Greece did the Romans finally establish themselves as peacemakers and assume direct governmental responsibility over Hellenistic Greece, no longer restricting themselves to the functions of a guarantor, benefactor and protector. Only after anarchy broke out and the bequeathed countries threatened to fall into the hands of potentially dangerous rivals did they finally take matters into their own hands and proceed towards establishing *provincias*.[2] After the province of Macedonia had already been created in 146 B.C. and Pompey had reshaped the Hellenistic east through a system of client kingdoms in 67/66 B.C., the Romans took several decades more to subject all Greece to their dominion in 27 B.C., when they turned the municipalities of mainland Greece into the province of Achaia.

In modern history, the United States accepted the need for permanent engagement on the old continent, ensuring the military protection, political reorganization and economic stabilization of Western Europe after 1945, when the nations of Europe had given evidence of their enduring inability to accomplish lasting peace and sustained political stability. At this point at the latest (faced with the prospect of Europe falling into the hands of the USSR), the Americans understood that they could no longer confine themselves to providing financial support and economic aid, and that American hegemony had to be based at last on more enduring, tangible and institutional forms including the establishment of NATO and the operation of permanent U.S. military bases on European soil. (As a matter of course, America is thus still in the stage of indirect rule and informal control, as it still seems a fairly distant prospect for the United States to incorporate

---

[1] E. Badian, *Roman Imperialism in the Late Republic*, Oxford 1968, 29-31.
[2] Badian, 36. See also E.S. Gruen, *The Hellenistic World and the Coming of Rome*, 2 volumes, Berkeley 1984; R.M. Kallet-Marx, *Hegemony to Empire. The Development of the Roman Imperium in the East from 148 to 62 B.C.*, Berkeley 1995.

the nations of Europe into its sovereign territory and control, making itself the formal leader of a united empire of the West.[1])

Yet at the end of the day, both the Romans during their republican period and the Americans in modern history have had a generally poor record as occupiers and colonizers. Even after the establishment of provinces since the middle of the second century B.C, the Romans left the job of systematic administrative penetration of the provinces and dependent territories undone throughout the republican period, pursuing only haphazard policies and waiting for the empire (from Augustus onwards) to subject the city's territorial acquisitions to a consistent system of government, administration and dense institutionalized reign.

As for the United States, the American people has consistently preferred, after almost every war since World War I, to demobilize as soon as possible and bring the troops home Generally speaking, America prefers to turn its attention to domestic issues rather than assuming the costs and pains of foreign occupation and nation-building. As Niall Ferguson has stated, the U.S. has persistent difficulties in turning short-term military victory into long-term political success and establishing viable civil structures and institutions. Anxious to "bring the boys home" as quickly as possible, the Americans are inclined to short-lived "hit and run" operations and tend to show little enthusiasm for political reconstruction and sustained institutional reorganization (the exceptions of course being the success stories of Germany and Japan, where the U.S. has also kept thousands of troops based ever since World War II.)

As Ferguson deplores, the Americans are eager to transfer sovereignty back to locals, install governments compatible with U.S. interests and withdraw their troops from occupied territories as swiftly as possible instead of shouldering the imperial responsibility and becoming engaged in nation-building in places like Afghanistan or Iraq. According to Ferguson, the Americans are reluctant in general to spend long times abroad and maintain prolonged presences in occupied countries, and hence tend to leave precipitately before economic reconstruction and political stabilization is achieved.

---

[1] Cf. Chapter 2.

Whereas "at Oxford and Cambridge a hundred years ago, ambitious students dreamed of ... embarking on careers in the British imperial administration," Ferguson laments, "the elite products of the Ivy League" do not aim to become imperial bureaucrats or govern Mesopotamia but rather "set their sights on business schools" as they dream of managing a hedge fund, a law firm or an investment bank. "Their dream is by definition an American dream."[1]

At the same time, America has been highly reluctant — in a manner structurally similar to the ancient Romans — to formally annex any territories outside their own immediate continent. When Santo Domingo offered itself for annexation in 1869, the proposal was defeated in Congress on the grounds that the U.S. Constitution did not empower the federal government to establish a colony. In the 1890s, President Grover Cleveland refused to annex Hawaii and attempted to restore the native queen as the representative of the indigenous population, much to the disappointment and outrage of the American residents and settlers who had toppled her to pave the way for the island's incorporation into the United States. When a draft annexation treaty was turned down in Congress for the second time, Theodore Roosevelt lamented "the queer lack of imperial instinct" shown and demonstrated by the American people.[2]

But why were (or are) the superpowers so reluctant to conquer, annex, and acquire territories and become entangled on a long-term basis in the matters and affairs of other nations, especially ancient Greece and modern Europe respectively? Why did (or do) they, for long periods of time, confine themselves to the roles of a peacemaker, arbitrator and guarantor, repeatedly withdrawing their victorious troops after having brought provisional stability and preliminary peace? Why were (or are) they so unwilling to extend their reach beyond the own borders and exercise direct governmental control over other nations until, in the case of ancient Rome, this turned out to be inevitable and virtually indispensable?

Again, the persistent reluctance of the superpowers to conquer and annex has much to do with their particular constitutional patriotism, i.e., the very special way, in which the Romans and Americans were (or are) committed to their republican constitutions, and by which

---

[1] Ferguson, 210.
[2] Cf. Ferguson, 93. It was only in 1898 that President William McKinley finally signed the annexation treaty.

they have stood out from any other power of their contemporary history and time. In fact, Roman history consistently revolved around the ideas of authority, tradition, constitution and foundation.[1] Over long periods of time, Roman politics remained intrinsically tied to the act of foundation, as the Romans stood in the unbroken tradition of what generations of ancestors had created and accomplished ever since the eighth century B.C. When the Americans established their own constitution at the end of the 18th century, they explicitly strove to resuscitate the spirit of ancient Rome and employed the Roman constitution as a model for their own republican fabrics.

Like the ancient Romans, the modern Americans also sought to ensure civic harmony through a system of checks and balances, separation of powers and mixed government structures with a combination of monarchical, aristocratic and democratic elements (the president or the consuls, the senate, the house of representatives or the plebeian assembly, and finally the office of the praetor as the highest-ranking legal officer and the Supreme Court or attorney general in the U.S.). In fact, the vocabulary of the American Revolution reverberated with echoes of republican Rome, as the revolutionaries aimed to emulate the guiding principles of the Roman constitution and state.

James Madison and Alexander Hamilton, two major contributors to the U.S. Constitution, not only sought to re-establish the "stupendous fabrics" of republican government once having bolstered the principle of liberty in ancient Rome but also published their ideas pseudonymously as "Publius" in the Federalist Papers (referring to Publius Valerius Poplicola, the legendary founder and first consul of the Roman republic).[2] Other agitators disputing pseudonymously in the papers of the American Revolution referred to themselves as

---

[1] At the same time, it has to be emphasized that the constitution of ancient Rome was not a single document, but rather a set of codified political rules and norms, deliberately open to evolvement and change. The basic element of the Roman constitution, which the American revolutionaries set out to emulate, was limited government in a system of checks and balances between the senate, the magistrates and the popular assembly, based on the principles of collegiality and tribunician intercession, and reflecting a class consensus established between the patricians and the plebeians since the end of the "Conflict of the Orders" in 287 B.C. Among other things, this constitutional compromise had strongly extended the plebeians' voting rights and eligibility for public office (see also Chapter 13 below).

[2] Mortimer N.S. Sellers, *American Republicans. Roman Ideology in the United States Constitution*, Basingstoke/New York 1994, 7ss.

"civis," "Cato" or "Brutus." When the members of the American citizen army returned to their homes and farms after the end of the War of Independence, they committed themselves to lasting republican values and called themselves the "Society of the Cincinnati" after Rome's famous general Lucius Quinctius Cincinnatus, who, as mentioned above, had returned to his plough after saving the republic as a 16-days' dictator in 458 B.C.[1]

By emulating Roman institutions like the Senate and places like the Capitol, the founding fathers aimed to provide the new constitutional framework with a degree of authority which they considered necessary to ensure its perpetuity, i.e., to found constitutional institutions with a prospect of being as lasting and enduring as those of the ancient Roman republic. Indeed, the durability of the Roman and American bodies politic, and the ways in which the Romans and Americans have worshipped their constitutions, vastly differ from the vicissitudes of ancient Greece and modern Europe, where one constitution has replaced another in quick succession. As in ancient Rome, the lastingness of the American constitution also originates from an act of foundation, to which American politics and history remain inseparably tied, including a set of constitutional amendments that refer to and augment the basic, original corpus of the constitution.

Taking into consideration this special constitutional relationship, however, a major reason underlying the sustained reluctance of the Romans and Americans to conquer, annex and establish direct imperial rule is to be seen in the fact that the exercise of imperial control over other nations and peoples has always tended to destroy the foundations and basic values of a republican constitution. As far back as ancient Greece, already Aristotle had warned of imperialist expansion as a fundamental threat to political freedom, since the imperial experience of limitless power would seduce rulers to seek unlimited power within the city itself as well.[2]

In fact, the Roman term of "imperator" originated back in the republican period, when it served to denote the largely unaccountable ruler and military commander of a province. Not by accident did

---

[1] Miner Myers, *Liberty without Anarchy. A History of the Society of the Cincinnati*, Charlottesville 1983.
[2] Arthur M. Eckstein, "Rome and the Hellenistic World: Masculinity and Militarism, Monarchy and Republic," in: David Tabachnick / Toivo Koivukoski (eds.), *Enduring Empire. Ancient Lessons for Global Politics*, Toronto 2009, 114-126, 119.

true republicans like Cato the Elder harshly criticize the policies of unaccountable foreign (or provincial) rule, including the ruthlessly humiliating treatment of Rhodes in 167 B.C. He even tried to sue the Roman commander Sulpicius Galba for massacring the Lusitanians, a Spanish tribe (who had already put down their arms) in 150 B.C. In a way, the true republicans understood that the disregard of limited government on the peripheries of the republic (i.e., the toleration of unaccountable, personal military commandos) raised the specter of tyranny and also posed a threat to the institutions of limited government within the republic itself.[1] Eventually, this is precisely what happened to Rome when Julius Caesar's unlimited (personal) commando, i.e., authority to operate outside the confines of the constitution in the Gallic periphery, led to the imposition of tyranny on Rome itself by Caesar and his professional, personally committed troops in 49 B.C.

As for modern America, already the political theorist John Caldwell Calhoun (1782–1850) was aware of the same threat when he warned his fellow countrymen that lawless rule on the fringes of America would finally undermine the rule of law within the United States itself.[2] In a speech delivered on the Mexican Cession in 1848, Calhoun warned that there was no "example on record of any free state holding a province ... without disastrous consequences. The nations conquered and held as a province have, in time, retaliated by destroying the liberty of their conquerors through the corrupting effect of extended patronage and irresponsible power." In fact, Calhoun explicitly referred to the history of ancient Rome, pointing out that when "Roman power passed beyond the limits of Italy, crossed the Adriatic, the Mediterranean and the Alps, liberty fell prostrate; the Roman people became a rabble; corruption penetrated every department of the government; violence and anarchy ruled the day, and military despotism closed the scene."[3]

In summary, it is therefore attributable not least to the devoted reverence for their constitutions that the Romans and Americans were (or are) so reluctant to pursue policies of annexation, foreign conquest and systematic establishment of imperial rule. Undoubtedly,

---

[1] Eckstein, 120.
[2] Eckstein, 115s.
[3] Quoted in David Edward Hendrickson, "In the Mirror of Antiquity: The Problem of American Empire," in: Tabachnick/Koivukoski (eds.), 3-19, 13.

the immediate subjugation of other nations and the exercise of direct governmental control would cut the bonds that tie American politics to the framework of the constitution, the balanced system of civic liberty and the original act of foundation. The basic fear shared by all true republicans, whether in ancient Rome or modern America, is that lawless rule on the outskirts of a nation that embarks on a policy of annexation and foreign conquest will eventually migrate back to the center, exhausting liberty and paving the way for despotism and tyrannical rule. Imperialism, as they have feared and suspected, is poised to destroy the strong sense of civic and constitutional liberty, by which the Roman and the American republic have stood out so remarkably from all other nations and powers of their respective ages and times.

From a certain point onwards, though, Rome's foreign policy ceased being guided by restraint and confined to security interests. Now it was characterized by increasingly "imperialist" practices of intransigence, aggression and exploitation.

In this respect, the watershed in Roman history, marking the start of the late republican period, was the Second Punic War followed by the victories over the large Hellenistic powers (the Macedonians and Seleucids), at the end of which Rome found itself in a lone superpower status in 201/190 B.C. After Carthage in particular had been disarmed and eliminated as a major political and military force, no serious geopolitical rival existed that the Romans had to fear or be concerned about. From this point onwards, Rome's foreign policy was now marked by an increasingly harsh and disdainful treatment of enemies, refractory kingdoms and recalcitrant allies.

In 171 B.C., Rome started the preventive Third Macedonian War (171–168) against King Perseus of Macedon, followed by the country's dismemberment into four independent republics after the crushing defeat of the Macedonians in the battle of Pydna in 168 B.C. After Pydna, the Romans were no longer ready to negotiate peace with Perseus as they had done with his father after the First and Second Macedonian Wars. Instead, the king was presented in a triumphal procession in the streets of Rome and he perished in a Roman dungeon, while 150,000 defeated Macedonians (or Epirotes) were put up and sold on the slave market.

Soon afterwards, Rome fought the deadly, ambush-stricken guerilla war in the woods and mountains of Spain from 153–133 B.C., in which traditional standards of warfare were abandoned and the Roman generals showed levels of atrocity, unwillingness to compromise, harsh enemy treatment, dishonorable warfare and disregard of peace treaties that shocked and appalled many long-standing senators.[1]

The complete destruction of Carthage came in 146 B.C., when it virtually was leveled to the ground. Its entire population was either killed or enslaved by Scipio Aemilianus in the aftermath of the Third Punic War, although the city, at that time, had long ceased representing a serious rival or strategic threat.

Also in 146 B.C., after the Achaean League had refused to obey a Roman order to dissolve, the Romans razed the city of Corinth to the ground in a spirit of previously unknown ferocity as an exemplary punishment indicating what would happen to any future insubordinate kingdom, nation or city-state.

The new intransigence was also reflected in the disdainful and humiliating treatment of Rome's long-standing allies like Rhodes and Pergamum after they failed to provide unambiguous support to Rome in its conflict with the Macedonians. In 144 B.C., Rhodes and Pergamum were stripped of commercial privileges, their rulers were humiliated, and the people of Pergamum were told by a Roman envoy that, from now on, any citizen dissatisfied with measures or actions of the king had the right to appeal to a Roman tribunal.

From the middle of the second century onwards, the Romans no longer showed their old generosity and restraint towards Hellenistic Greece but quickly proceeded to the establishment and large-scale exploitation of provinces, which became subjects of immoderate lawless rule. In 146 B.C., Rome turned Macedonia into one of its first provinces proper, followed by Asia Minor in 129, Cilicia in 78, Bithynia in 74 and Syria in 64 B.C. As we shall see in Chapter 13, the acquisition of provinces soon set the stage for excessive exploitation, as huge amounts of money were squeezed out of the newly acquired lands, and for the rise of unaccountable self-serving provincial rulers (like Pompey and Caesar) as the new makers and shakers of Rome's domestic policy.

---

[1] Pearson, 93s.

As for present-day America, U.S. foreign policies have likewise shifted from defensive motivations to increasingly unilateral, belligerent and uncompromising practices since the fall and implosion of the USSR in 1991. In asserting the superpower's dominant role in world affairs, the United States has developed a growing inclination to disregard international law, reflected in the interventions in Yugoslavia without a U.N. mandate in the 1990s and then, most strikingly, in 2003 when the Bush administration set out to attack Iraq although the U.N. Security Council had refused to authorize the invasion.

However, the United States has not only become inclined to bypass international institutions and disregard international agreements if U.S. interests require, it has also shown a disconcerting inclination to lawless, classically "imperialist" practices, especially since 9/11/2001. Among other things, this includes the establishment of secret prisons in Eastern Europe and aggressive interrogation centers like Guantanamo, Bagram (the main prison facility in Afghanistan), and Abu Ghraib in Iraq, in which the rule of law has been suspended and a new category of "illegal enemy combatants" have been subjected to unaccountable forms of punitive treatment. In particular, captives from the battlefields of Afghanistan and Iraq have been denied POW status and have been held in animal cages, as the U.S. claims their treatment is not subject to either international or constitutional safeguards and constraints. At the same time, U.S. forces have flown detainees to countries with questionable human rights records like Egypt or Uzbekistan, where interrogators are not accountable to any regular U.S. jurisdiction.

Not by accident have terms and concepts from Rome's imperial past become increasingly popular in recent years to describe the conducts and practices of U.S. foreign policy. Already in 2000, General Anthony Zinni, then commander in chief of the U.S. Central Command, told a journalist that he "had become a modern-day proconsul, descendant of the warrior-statesmen who once ruled the Roman Empire's outlying territory ..."[1] In 2003/2004, Paul Bremer as U.S. ambassador to Iraq and head of the Coalition Provisional Authority (CPA) was explicitly referred to as the "proconsul" (the ancient Roman governors presiding over a Roman province), i.e., as a person ruling not through laws but

---

[1] Cf. Ferguson, 6.

rather, along classically imperialist lines, through ordinances and decrees.[1]

At the same time, the respect shown by the superpower for its long-standing allies has also declined significantly, in a manner similar to Rome's rising disregard of its oldest allies in Greece like Pergamum or Rhodes. In the run-up to the war on Iraq, U.S. government representatives, diplomats and senators not only spoke disparagingly of "old Europe" but made it clear to recalcitrant allies like the Germans that disobedience would have unpleasant consequences. In particular, Germany was warned that the U.S. would consider moving its military bases (along with the related civilian jobs for locals) away to more loyal vassal nations in Eastern Europe.

In the early second century B.C., the Romans developed a firm conviction "that they had a calling to rule the world."[2] Similarly, U.S. Secretary of State Madeleine Albright made no attempt in 1998 to hide Americas' fundamental sense of superiority, i.e., the fact that United States saw a fundamental difference in value and rank between itself and its allies: "If we have to use force, it is because we are America. We are the indispensable nation. We stand tall and we see further than other countries into the future."[3]

Risen to a colossus "no longer bound by international law, the concerns of allies or constraints on its military force,"[4] the United States — like Rome since the early second century B.C. — has shown an increased readiness to crush any nation daring to defy the superpower, to offer resistance, to challenge its hegemony. In other words, the U.S. shows an inclination to consider any opposition basically illegitimate and a determination to no longer deal with enemies and foes but only with villains, rebels and rogues deserving punishment and destruction.[5] No longer accepting anybody else as equal, the Romans and Americans, after their rise to lone superpower status, tend to disregard the natural security interests, cultural

---

[1] Jeremy Scahill, *Blackwater. The Rise of the World's Most Powerful Mercenary Army*, London 2007, 47. A similar function has also been ascribed to David Petraeus (cf. Cames Lord, *Proconsuls: Delegated Political-Military Leadership from Rome to America Today*, New York 2012).
[2] Bender, *The New Rome*, 84.
[3] As quoted in Oliver Stone / Peter Kuznick, *The Concise Untold History of the United States*, London 2014, 272.
[4] Chalmers Johnson, *The Sorrows of Empire. Militarism, Secrecy and the End of the Republic*, New York 2004, 3.
[5] Bender, *The New Rome*, 88.

identities and historical traditions of resistive powers or nations (such as Russia, Libya or Iraq in the case of America) and show a steadily decreasing willingness to compromise or make concessions.

Instead, they become determined to actively extend their informal empires and fasten their grips on ever more distant regions such as Spain, Gaul, Asia Minor and North Africa in the case of Rome, and the Middle East, Eurasia and the former Soviet republics in the case of the United States — along with the systematic expansion of NATO right to the Russian border. Like the Romans who were determined after the Second Punic War to never permit the rise again of any rival threatening their geopolitical predominance, security and survival, and who felt justified to launch pre-emptive strikes against any potentially ascending power, Paul Wolfowitz declared in 2002 that America would now seek "full spectrum dominance of the planet"[1] and that "America's political and military mission in the post-Cold War era [would] be to ensure that no rival superpower is allowed to emerge in Western Europe, Asia, or the territory of the former Soviet Union ... a world where there is one dominant military power whose leaders must deter competitors from even aspiring to a larger regional or global role."[2]

Since the fall of the USSR and America's rise to lone superpower status, U.S. foreign policies have become increasingly unilateral, willing to disregard international law (including the obligation to observe the Geneva Convention) and act without consideration for the concerns of allies or opposing nations when it comes to the assertion of global pre-eminence and domination — in a manner structurally similar to how the Romans acted after the elimination of any relevant strategic rival since the early second century B.C.

At the end of the day, it looks as though the rise to lone superpower status unleashed the expansionary energies of both the Romans and Americans which, until then, had been held in check by republican instincts of restraint.[3] In ancient Rome, we see an advancing trend since

---

[1] Chalmers Johnson, *Nemesis. The Last Days of the American Republic*, New York 2006, 138.

[2] As quoted in Johnson, *Nemesis*, 58.

[3] The fact that "Washington's policies have become gradually more stringent since the Soviet Union ceased to exist" is also acknowledged by Bender, *The New Rome*, 86. The watershed in Roman history was not, however, as Bender holds, the Third Punic War against the already fundamentally enfeebled Carthaginians, but the Second Punic War and the defeat of the large Hellenistic powers in 197 and 190 B.C. respectively.

the second century B.C. (i.e., in the late republican years) of wars of conquest being unleashed for interests of personal fame and financial enrichment through foreign exploitation — from the subjugation of Gaul, Spain and the smaller Hellenistic kingdoms right down to the cataclysmic campaign against the Parthians, ending in the ultimate defeat and death of Crassus in 53 B.C. In modern history, the U.S. too has felt liberated from former considerations and constraints after its rise to sole superpower status.

The Bush administration in particular developed the idea of preventive war and regime change, i.e., the forcible removal of governments and the installation of pro-American, pro-market governments in countries which had not attacked or threatened to attack the United States. They were determined to bring democracy and free enterprise — as the only tolerable route by which nations can prosper — to every corner of the world, if necessary by military force. Under a new concept of national security developed by Cheney and Bush, security was no longer limited to self-defense or to the suppression of genuine threats, and the U.S. no longer paid respect to the sovereign rights of other nations. Instead, any nation in the world became the potential target of a pre-emptive military strike and regime change operation.

The "National Security Strategy of the United States of America" of September 17, 2002, asserted the right of the United States to use military force anywhere in the world, at any time it chooses and against any country it believes could become a future threat to vital U.S. interests, i.e., any country potentially developing weapons of mass destruction or potentially providing support to terrorists.

At the same time, the United States has shown significantly less consideration and been substantially more forceful in pushing through its own economic principles and interests: In an unprecedentedly radical approach unthinkable before, Paul Bremer as head of the Coalition Provisional Authority (CPA) in Iraq implemented a sweeping program of liberalization and free enterprise in the occupied country in 2003/04. He dismantled almost the entire public sector (including the layoff of 500,000 government employees) and provided for the privatization of Iraq's 200 largest state-owned public businesses and utility companies and their sale to transnational corporations. Under Bremer's agenda, the Iraqi economy was opened to foreign investment and trade without import tariffs and export duties, and foreign companies and banks were allowed to take 100% of their profits out of the country without having to pay taxes. Along with laws prohibiting trade unions and collective bargaining, this made Iraq "a capitalist dream," fulfilling the wishes of U.S. investors (or contractors) and neoclassical economists without respect of Iraq's national interests and traditions.

In conclusion, it is still a reassuring fact on the one hand that U.S. army staff involved in classically "imperialist" behaviors like torture, physical coercion, sexual humiliation and prisoner abuse, as they occurred most prominently in the Abu Ghraib prison complex in Iraq in 2003, are still prosecuted and convicted by the political, military and judicial authorities in the United States. The willingness to prosecute and hold those responsible (although apparently only the lower ranks) to judicial account provides indication that the spirit of the American republic is still intact in principle and that the United States is still willing to maintain the fundamental values of its constitutional order.

Nevertheless, the new signs of intransigence, the increasingly uncompromising nature of U.S. foreign policy, the lawless practices and the abandonment of former considerations and constraints suggest that the U.S. after the fall of the USSR could be following the course of Rome after its rise to unrivalled superpower status in the early second century B.C. Clearly, the aggressive policies and lawless practices pursued in recent years by the United States are warning signs that America may, after all, follow the trajectory of Rome and be about to enter into the early stages of a pre-imperial development, as the ancient Roman republic did since the early second century B.C.[1]

The lessons of the ancient Roman experience warn that this represents a dangerous course, as a consequence of which the principles of lawful government and republican liberty (the rule of law) may one day be sacrificed for the sake of global supremacy and the hegemonic accumulation of power. (The very circumstance that America has readily been described as an empire in intellectual debates, especially after 9/11/2001, and that such descriptions have

---

[1] Another development pointing in this direction can be seen in the unilateral (pre-imperial) extension of U.S. jurisdiction, for instance, to Swiss taxation practices or the FIFA corruption charges, with international soccer officials facing arrest on FBI warrants and investigations.

not met with more massive resistance, may be seen as a warning sign. As Charles S. Maier has stated, "the very idea of Empire would have caused righteous indignation amongst U.S. observers" a few decades ago on the grounds of America's anti-imperial origins and self-conception.[1])

Taking into account that the United States was forged in a war of independence against imperial rule and born out of opposition to an empire — and given that empire was long regarded by the Americans as the epitome of militarism, corruption and excess as opposed to republican virtue — the recent praise of empire may well be a warning as to what the future has in store for America and what threats its republican spirit and constitutional values may have to face.

NOTE ON RUSSIA

Despite a number of substantial differences, striking parallels can be found between the role of Macedonia in ancient history and the role of Russia in modern times. In both cases, a fringe nation on the outskirts of Greece and Europe respectively, socially and economically underdeveloped and long regarded as only semi-civilized by the mainland Greeks and Europeans, finally pursued a policy of extensive modernization, turned into a looming threat to the city or nation states, and subjected parts of Greece and Europe respectively to its dominion.

In the further course, the Macedonians and the Russians challenged the emergent superpowers of Rome and the United States — which, for their part, assumed the role of guarantor and protector of the Greeks and Europeans (and their freedom) in view of the Macedonian or Soviet threat.

Finally, however, the Macedonians and the Russians were defeated and disempowered by the Romans in the course of three

---

[1] Charles S. Meier as quoted in Cox, 23. For America's description as an empire, cf. Chapter 2. In a particularly outspoken manner, the conservative American intellectual Robert Kaplan made the case for empire as "the most benign of all political systems" and argued that America should study the Roman Empire "for hints about how to run American foreign policy." (Robert Kaplan, *Warrior Politics. Why Leadership Demands a Pagan Ethos*, New York 2002, 152ss.) In fact, Kaplan even praised the emperor Tiberius for his combination of prudent diplomacy and the use of violence to preserve a peace conducive to the interests of Rome.

Macedonian wars (214–168 B.C.) and by America in 1989/91, when the Soviet Union disintegrated after its defeat in the Cold War, and Russia renounced its claim over Eastern Europe as Macedon once had to waive its claim over Greece in 197 B.C.

As for Macedonia, the Antigonid dynasty was deposed and the kingdom of Macedon divided into four puppet tributary republics in 168 B.C., before the Roman province of Macedonia was finally established in 146 B.C. When strategic circles in the administration of George H. W. Bush nurtured the idea of splitting Russia into four separate entities and in this way to discard it as a major power in 1991, it almost seems as though someone in the U.S. administration had carefully studied the history books. Judging by the analogy with ancient Rome, there is much to suggest that the United States would not have allowed Russia to remain an independent nation and, to some extent, an antagonist strategic force (and autonomous actor) if it had not been for Russia's possession of nuclear weapons. On the other hand, the Russians ought to learn from history and the deplorable fate of the Macedonian kings that, whatever they do, they should not try to challenge the superpower and dare to defy its vastly superior military, economic, financial and cultural might.

13. Present-Day America and Late Republican Rome

The central question to be explored when comparing present-day America with late republican Rome is whether any structural trends can be identified in current U.S. politics, society and culture that carry echoes of what happened two thousand years ago, in the late years of the Roman republic, i.e., the period of ancient history structurally corresponding to the present stage of Western (or occidental) history.

Are there any signs that America's republican institutions or, even more importantly, the social, economic and cultural foundations underlying the constitutional framework and republican institutions of the United States, are facing challenges similar to those which once threatened (and eventually undermined) the stability and vigor of the Roman republic in the second and first century B.C.? (Or, in other words: are there any indications that the United States is following a course similar to that of the Roman society and state in the late republican period?)

As a matter of course, we must be careful here to avoid precipitate conclusions, as the power of America is still young and vigorous, and the institutional strength and republican spirit of the United States is still essentially intact. After all, it remains a tenable view that present-day America will overcome its current imbalances and afflictions, just as the Roman republic passed through a number of serious crises before the one of the first century B.C. eventually proved fatal.

As the American Civil War and the Great Depression show, crisis and decline can also have the capacity to bring renewal, mobilize fresh energy and provide new cohesion. Nevertheless, given that the social, political and economic predicaments of present-day America bear striking resemblance to those once having afflicted late republican Rome, it makes sense to compare the two historical periods and take the fate of late republican Rome as a warning for what America may face if it fails to reverse some current social, economic and politics trends and find ways of establishing new forms of social, economic and political equilibrium.

LATE REPUBLICAN ROME

Indeed, both late republican Rome and present-day America were (or are) periods of excessive financial speculation and mounting social polarization. Whereas the early Roman economy was still a subsistence economy run by small artisans and peasants on the basis of agrarian self-sufficiency, the late republic since the early second century B.C. saw a concentration of capital and accumulation of wealth in the hands of a few.[1]

On the estates of large landed proprietors, a rationalized, market-oriented villa and pasture economy came into being after the Second Punic War, which focused on large-scale, specialized agricultural production and international trade, making systematic use of free agricultural labor and a steadily rising number of slaves. While the Roman economy underwent increased marketization and monetization since the early second century B.C., many small independent farmers were displaced and expelled from their ancestral lands, which passed into the hands of large estate proprietors. Increasingly, the small landholders, artisans and farmers, who had once formed the supporting pillars of the Roman society and state, saw themselves reduced to a dispossessed proletarian mass, as

---

[1] John K. Davies, "Hellenistic Economies," in: Bugh (ed.), 73-92, 80. Works of reference for the history of Rome in general and the late republican period in particular include: Peter A. Brunt, *The Fall of the Roman Republic and related essays*, Oxford 1988; E. Badian, *Roman Imperialism in the Late Republic*, Oxford 1968; Mary Beard / Michael Crawford, *Rome in the Late Republic: Problems and Interpretations*, London 1999; Klaus Bringmann, *Krise und Ende der römischen Republik (133-42 v. Chr.)*, Berlin 2003; Karl Christ, *Das Römische Weltreich. Aufstieg und Zerfall einer antiken Großmacht*, Freiburg/Basel/Wien 1973; John Boardman / Jasper Griffin / Oswyn Murray (eds.), *The Oxford History of the Roman World*, Oxford 1991; Harriet E. Flower (ed.), *The Cambridge Companion to the Roman Republic*, Cambridge 2004.

social polarization was aggravated and the concentration of wealth progressed.

As a result of Rome's military victories over the great Hellenistic powers and its conquest of the Greek east, booty and war compensations poured into Rome, along with precious metals, luxury goods, and the riches of exploited provinces and tributary kingdoms. The denarius soon became the world's leading currency, and Rome established itself as the unrivalled financial center of the ancient world.[1] (As a result of Rome's victorious campaigns in Greece in 200–190 B.C. alone, the Macedonian and Seleucid kings had to pay indemnities of 10,000 and 15,000 silver talents respectively, totaling 1.25 million pounds. After the battle of Pydna in 168 B.C., the palace of the Macedonian kings was plundered and gold, art, jewelry and precious stones were carried through the streets of Rome in more than 250 wagons in a triumphal celebration lasting several days.)

Gradually, a new elite of capitalists, speculators, merchants and bankers emerged who indulged in provocative luxury and no longer adhered to the traditional, conservative style of the patricians. The new monetized elite — i.e., the senatorial and equestrian nobility who usurped the lion's share of the steady inflow of capital and precious metal into Rome — no longer showed the old moderation in the use of wealth and ceased granting the traditional economic and political protection to the plebs. Instead, they began investing heavily in agricultural land, as a result of which the plebs lost large parts of their ancestral property and were gradually transformed into a mass of "rootless pauperized proletarians."[2]

For their large-scale construction, infrastructure, water supply and sanitation projects, the new, immensely rich class of private entrepreneurs made extensive use of slave and free urban labor. While building and construction speculators like Crassus celebrated triumphs in the late republican years, the unpropertied masses, to which many of the former artisans, shopkeepers and freehold farmers had been reduced (but which also included large numbers of foreigners and liberated slaves), lived in the miserable conditions of their urban tenement houses.

---

[1]   A. Schulten, "Roman Cruelty and Extortion," in: Erich Gruen (ed.), *Imperialism in the Roman Republic*, New York 1970, 60-66.
[2]   Stockton, 28.

By contrast to the old plebs, the new urban proletariat no longer enjoyed the traditional shelter under the clientela system. In the heyday of the republic, that system had granted socio-economic protection to ordinary people — based on the client's obligation to serve and support his patron in political and electoral affairs — and ensured their integration into Rome's social and political life despite its domination in principle by a wealthy aristocratic elite.[1]

At the same time, the artisans and peasants of the Italian peninsula saw their economic basis collapse as a result of Rome's rise to global supremacy and unrivalled economic control of the Mediterranean after the Second Punic War. Increasingly, Rome's military victories in the east and south led to a massive influx of slaves, with 150,000 Epirotes alone being captured by Roman troops, as mentioned above, and put on the slave market in 167 B.C. In fact, the traditional plebs was increasingly deprived of its economic basis and rendered superfluous, as the new, powerful class of capitalists, merchants, financial speculators and large landed proprietors made large-scale use of slave labor, and substantial shares of Rome's domestic production, previously provided by the artisans and peasants, were no longer required due to cheap imports of food and other products from the subjected regions of Greece, Spain, North Africa and Asia Minor. (In the early first century B.C., annual imports included 10 million sacks of grain alone from Egypt and Spain.)

The concentration of land ownership in combination with the operation of large landed estates or plantations with slave labor pressurized the class of small independent farmers who had once formed the backbone of the Roman society, state and citizen army. As the previous class of plebeians (i.e., small landholders, artisans and farmers) was transformed into economically useless proletarians, extreme social polarization resulted between the dispropertied urban masses and a predatory class of plutocrats.

At the same time, atomization and civic disconnection spread among the dispossessed urban population, which felt less and less committed to the state and its political, social and religious institutions. No longer an independent political actor like the old,

---

[1] The clientela system is therefore explicitly referred to by Monte L. Pearson as "a social safety net in a world where governments did not provide welfare or social security" (Monte L. Pearson, *Perils of Empire. The Roman Republic and the American Republic*, New York 2008, 48).

traditional plebs (with its bonds of solidarity and experience of joint, collective political action), the impoverished masses sought distraction, entertainment and relaxation at the games (in the arena), becoming progressively dependent on the sponsoring of meals or dinner parties by political candidates and the free supply of grain, which the proletarian population of Rome was legally entitled to receive from 59 B.C. onwards.

Whereas the Law of the Twelve Tables — augmented by the social and constitutional compromise legislation passed in 367 B.C. — had included effective regulations for the protection of debtors, artisans and farmers, a ban on seaborne trading by the senatorial elite, and restrictions regarding luxury food, interest rates and precious metal possession,[1] the late, "pre-imperial" republic was marked by sweeping deregulation and the unlimited reign of money. In terms of public life, political careers came to require immense financial resources to make the electoral donations and fund the indispensable canvassing meals, dinner parties, festivals and games. In fact, the entire political process was increasingly monetized, as billionaires like Crassus spent millions of denars to ensure electoral victory of their handpicked candidates for the offices of consul, praetor, quaestor, censor and tribune of the plebs.

In late republican Rome, money completely dominated the political sphere, as candidates could not succeed without vast financial resources from the millionaires and billionaires to wage their electoral campaigns and pay the electoral bribes. (As a matter of fact, the distribution of money to voters on behalf of candidates became a profession of its own, assumed by the *divisors* or money allocation agents, who bore strong structural resemblance to modern fundraising organizations in the United States.)

At the same time, progressive monetization of the public sphere was also reflected in the fact that the publicani, i.e., private entrepreneurs, financiers and tax collectors who partly merged into huge leasing corporations over the course of the first and second century B.C., took over more and more public functions such as construction, coal and silver mine operation, salt refineries, army and navy victualling and war material supplies. As a consequence, a new class of wealthy merchants and publicans of equestrian rank rose to

---

[1] Jean-Jacques Aubert, "The republican economy and Roman law: regulation, promotion and reflection?," in: Flower (ed.), 160-178, 164-169.

immense political influence. For the years around and after 100 B.C., we know from inscriptions that many Italian cities resorted to public contracting with private entrepreneurs not only for army supplies and tax collection but also for the construction of roads, ports and other public buildings and for law enforcement purposes, including the infliction of capital punishment on convicted criminals and slaves.[1]

Against the backdrop of galloping monetization and social polarization, the long-standing social and political compromise between the patricians and the plebeians, on which the stability and durability of the republic had rested, was progressively undermined, especially since the second half of the second century B.C. Instead, the governing elite now known as the *optimates* developed increasingly uncompromising attitudes, dissociating itself from the other sections of society and striving for personal enrichment without respect of the interests and concerns of the middle and lower class.

As the rich elite gave precedence to self-interest over civic unity, social concord and the common good, the traditional alliance between the patricians and the plebeians began to crumble. In particular, the ruling nobility became increasingly determined not to accept any social and political reform which might have restored the inherited culture of compromise and conciliation. Instead, the senatorial establishment and the wealthy knights not only closed their ranks and made sure that new senators, consuls and magistrates came only from the highest ranks (or richest sections) of society, they also secluded themselves on large villa estates furnished and ornamented with Greek statues, sculptures, mosaics, colonnades and wall paintings which their proprietors collected as status symbols and means of class distinction.

Showing no readiness for the re-establishment of social compromise, the ruling elite repeatedly turned down reform proposals aimed at the creation of small farming plots for members of the dispossessed urban population (most prominently for a distribution of the *ager publicus* in favor of the plebeians and to the disfavor of speculators and large landed proprietors, as proposed by the Gracchi brothers in 133 and 123 B.C.). Time and again, conservative resistance to social reform prevailed, as the members of the nobility-dominated senate were

---

[1] Aubert, 174.

busy buying small farms to enlarge their villa estates and were hence afraid of confiscation.

Ever since the futile attempt by Tiberius Gracchus to reclaim at least some land from the most prosperous families, the political life of Rome became increasingly disruptive, as conservative tribunes vetoed land reform bills and progressive tribunes vetoed, on certain occasions, every piece of official business in the city, halting public finances, trials and even meetings of the Senate.[1] (Since the assassination of the Gracchi, social conflict surrounding debt relief and land reform turned ever more violent until a series of civil wars finally broke out in the first century B.C. The rule of law, once so proudly hailed by the Romans, gave way to practices of assassination, proscription and gang fights, and a few titans like Sulla, Marius, Pompey and Caesar came to completely dominate the political stage.)

In fact, the suppression of agrarian reform continued throughout the last decades of the Roman republic down to the fierce resistance put up by Cicero — as the representative of the propertied classes during his consulship in 63 B.C. — against a land distribution bill, which had also provided for debt relief and a modest redistribution of wealth.[2] Claiming that debtors were victims only of their own idleness and otiosity, Cicero and the aristocrats disregarded the adverse conditions of the Italian peasantry, the widespread misery, desperation and distress among poor countrymen, tenant farmers, craftspeople, laborers and the unpropertied, landless masses, as they closed their minds and refused to respond to the need for social remedy and economic reform.[3] In the end, however, the sustained refusal of the governing elite to pass and accept reform deprived the republic of any reasonable chance to restore civic harmony between the estates and thus maintain what had been the city's greatest strength, i.e., a set of joint moral and civic values shared by all sections of society.

In particular, the reforms proposed by the Gracchi and other tribunician leaders also had a military purpose. They aimed to maintain the republican and popular character of the army by supporting and restoring the small farmers and peasant population, which had always been the core of the Roman army and was now facing ruin due to the seemingly unstoppable growth of large landed

---

[1] Pearson, 204.
[2] Stockton, 86s.
[3] Stockton, 105ss.

estates. The proposals for reform were also aimed at raising the population of small landowners and thus increasing the number of property-owning men who could serve in the legions, i.e., the number of citizens qualifying as Roman soldiers on the basis of their tax and census rating.

Yet instead of recovering the traditional civic unity and social concord, the elites chose to systematically deprive the plebs of its ability to act as an independent, self-assured political force. Under the constitutional revisions implemented by Sulla in 82–79 B.C., the tribunes of the plebs, i.e., the once mighty political representatives of the lower classes, were stripped of their right to submit legislative motions and propose new laws to the plebeian assembly without prior approval from the Senate. In addition, any elected tribune was now banned from running for any higher political office in the future, as a result of which the tribunate became a political dead end and an unattractive perspective for any politically ambitious and capable man. (Although some of its competencies were later restored, the tribunate never regained its former authority and weight.)

On top of this, the trade and neighborhood clubs once employed by the plebs for purposes of political organization and mobilization were effectively prohibited in the first century B.C. Stripped of their political power, the plebeians — which had once played a major constitutional role as a self-assured political factor and pillar of the Roman state — finally slipped into dependency and became increasingly corrupted by games, electoral bribes and the free or subsidized supply of grain.

In the further course of the first century B.C, however, the failure of the governing elite to acknowledge the interests and concerns of the peasantry, the middle classes and the poor[1] eventually took its toll on the civil liberties and constitutional foundations of the republic itself. As a consequence of rising inequality and mounting social polarization, it finally became impossible to retain the old connection between military service and land ownership, i.e., the principle that Roman soldiers had to be men of property, obliged to buy their own weapons and armor. Ever since the extensive army reform put in place by Marius in 107 B.C., property was no longer a

---

[1] Cf. Stockton, 30, who explicitly refers to the "exclusiveness and selfishness of the ruling oligarchy" in the late decades of the Roman Republic.

necessary qualification to become a legionary, and the ranks of the legions were filled with members of the dispossessed plebs and urban proletariat who volunteered for service. Before long, however, the new unpropertied soldiers lost any sense of loyalty to the institutions of the state, and the pride of serving the nation (or actively shaping and embodying the Roman state) declined. Instead, they came to rely entirely on their respective general or commander, who they hoped would provide them with a piece of land to make a living after the end of their military service careers.[1]

For the new type of soldier, the military service function changed from a public task into an essentially private relationship. At the same time, the new recruitment conditions enabled generals to pursue their own, private political agendas, increasingly emancipating themselves from subordination to the institutions of the state, i.e., the senate and magistrates of Rome. To make things worse, the dispossessed masses — stripped of the old plebeian ability to take collective political action and bring their influence to bear as an independent political force — eventually turned their backs on the institutions of the republic and sought salvation from Julius Caesar as the "man of the people," on whom the popular basis finally pinned its hopes after all attempts of socio-economic reform within the established republican structures had failed.

Eventually, in the atmosphere of polarization and unwillingness to compromise that marked especially the first century B.C., only authoritarian monocratic rule seemed capable of achieving the necessary social pacification and reconciliation. In the end, it appeared as though only Caesar was ready to grant the ordinary people what a wealthy elite had consistently denied them in more than a century of political antagonism and social conflict: whilst preserving property rights, the social order and the hierarchy itself, Caesar passed a comprehensive debt remission scheme which disburdened wide sections of the lower and middle classes of their severe financial distress. In addition, he made a massive attempt (already during his consulship in 59 B.C.) to solve Rome's long-standing conflict about property and land when he implemented a Farmland Act — despite stiff resistance from the senate and the wealthy elite — under which 20,000 impecunious, pauperized citizens of Rome were given the

---

[1] David Potter, *The Roman Army and Navy*, in: Flower, 66-88, 73, 81.

opportunity to settle as freehold farmers in the southern Italian region of Capua. In particular, Caesar saw to it that the plebeian assembly passed land reform legislation which gave fertile acreage in Campania to any Roman man who had three or more children.

During his entire consul- and dictatorship, Caesar not only provided for public works and grain supply to sustain the livelihood of the impoverished urban masses, he also founded and established more than 30 colonies in Southern Italy, Spain, France, the Balkans, Greece, Minor Asia and North Africa, providing land to more than 80,000 members of Rome's proletarian population.

Early 21st-Century America — Social Polarization

Turning our focus, at this point, to the circumstances and conditions of early 21st-century America, we can indeed observe a number of developments strongly reminiscent of what occurred two thousand years ago in late republican Rome. Like the social polarization seen in the late stages of the Roman republic between the urban masses and an increasingly plutocratic elite, extreme levels of inequality and social segregation have emerged as well in 21st-century America. As shown above, wide sections of the peasant and artisan population that once formed the supporting pillars of the Roman society and state saw themselves displaced, politically disempowered and dispossessed of their ancestral lands since the beginning of the second century B.C. In a structurally similar way, wide sections of the middle class and blue-collar workforce, which once formed the supporting pillars of U.S. society, are under heavy pressure in present-day America as the income gap between a rich elite and the mass of middle and working class employees has steadily widened.

Most strikingly, mounting social division is reflected in a drastic polarization of salaries and wages: while a chief executive earned 30 times the average wage of a skilled employee in 1970, this figure soared to 300 times the average wage of a skilled employee in 2010. Between 1990 and 2006, the average salary of a CEO rose by 600% (not including bonuses and stock options), while the top tax rate dropped from 70 to 35 percent and the capital income tax rate decreased from 35 to 15 percent.

By contrast, the average real income of manufacturing workers and white-collar employees was down by 28% during the same period of time. Moreover, the trend to inequality has been further fuelled by political decisions ever since Ronald Reagan's Economic Recovery Tax Act, which explicitly benefited the very wealthy sections of society in 1981. As Joseph Stieglitz has pointed out in the *Price of Inequality*, the entire increase in national wealth generated since the year 1990 has been absorbed by the 1% wealthiest Americans.[1]

EMPIRES OF CONSUMPTION

The artisans and peasants of Rome saw their economic basis collapse in the first and second century B.C. as a result of cheap imports of grain and other products from dependent and subjugated nations. Just so, millions of U.S. manufacturing jobs have been outsourced since the late 1980s to low-cost countries like China or Bangladesh — or moved over the border to Mexico under the NAFTA trade and investment agreement, which has proved to be a very effective instrument since 1994 to put pressure on the U.S. working class.

In fact, foreign low-cost competition has wiped out large parts of America's manufacturing sector, which now accounts for less than 10% of U.S. GDP. Like the Roman plebeians who were rendered economically dispensable through slave labor and cheap imports in the second century B.C., the U.S. manufacturing class is being made superfluous by imported foreign production, outsourcing and the relocation of jobs overseas. Just as many ordinary Romans slipped into debt bondage in the late republican years, America's middle class is haunted by indebtedness, mortgaged homes, car loans, and high costs for health care and university tuitions.

As Chris Hedges points out in *The Empire of Illusion*, America has been systematically shifting ever since the late 1980s from an empire of production to an "empire of consumption."[2] This indicates the strong structural resemblance between present-day America and late republican Rome, whose inhabitants likewise changed from being producers to consumers of imported foreign production in the first and second century B.C. In both cases, the domestic creation of value

---

[1] Joseph Stieglitz, *Price of Inequality. How Today's Divided Society Endangers Our Future*, New York 2012.
[2] Chris Hedges, *The Empire of Illusion. The End of Literacy and the Triumph of Spectacle*, New York 2009, 150s.

was (or is) replaced with the consumption of foreign production and the progressive influx of funds and goods from abroad.

In the history of antiquity, Rome established itself as the unrivalled financial center of the world and a new class of speculators and financial entrepreneurs emerged in the second century B.C. In parallel, the financial industry in the United States has seen spectacular growth ever since the 1980s, and it gradually gained predominance over all other economic sectors.

In fact, a new class of financial oligarchs has emerged in present-day America, which works with the profits generated through cheap, mainly offshore labor, large parts of which flow back into U.S. treasury bonds or dollar-denominated securities and flood the American equity market. (This also means that the staggering U.S. trade and budget deficits are financed through a constant inflow of capital from the outside world into the United States, absorbed by the American equity and government bond markets and hence funding U.S. government borrowing and private consumption.)[1] While the share of the financial industry in domestic U.S. corporate profits did not exceed 16% until 1985, that figure oscillated between 20 and 30% in 1990–2000 before soaring to 41% in the decade from 2001–2010.[2]

In ancient Rome, the shift from production to consumption and the continued influx of foreign funds was an immediate consequence of the city's rise to superpower status and unrivalled control of the Mediterranean world. From this point onwards, the Romans not only obtained huge amounts of money from booty, tribute and war compensation, they also could afford to rely on imports from Asia Minor, Spain and, in particular, Egypt as the famous *granary of Rome*, rather than on domestic production.

In modern times, America's rise to unrivalled global economic, political and military supremacy, especially since the collapse of the Soviet bloc in 1989/91, likewise seems to have enticed the United States into shifting the core of its economy from production to financial services, as its dominance over the globe (including the global

---

[1] That is why Yanis Varoufakis has called America the Global Minotaur, devouring the financial resources of the world, although a metaphor from the Roman context might have been more accurate historically than one from Greece's Minoan Age (Yanis Varoufakis, *The Global Minotaur. America, Europe and the Future of the Global Economy*, New York 2013).

[2] For this complex, see Simon Johnson, *13 Bankers. The Wall Street Takeover and the Next Financial Meltdown*, New York 2011.

economy) and its role as the unrivalled financial center of the world allow it to rely on imported production and a seemingly unstoppable flow of incoming funds from the world of cheap, especially Asian, labor.

THE DECLINE OF THE MIDDLE CLASS AND THE ABANDONMENT OF SOCIAL COMPROMISE

In universal history terms, the "assault on the middle and working class"[1] in early 21st-century America bears striking resemblance as well to what occurred 2000 years ago in the late stages of the Roman republic, highlighting the severe extent to which the economic and social foundations underlying America's republican inheritance are challenged, threatened and jeopardized. Just as the governing elite of ancient Rome weakened, disempowered or eliminated the inherited institutions of the plebs (the neighborhood associations and the institution of the tribunate of the plebs), the elite of power and money in America has launched a massive assault on the system of organized labor and the New Deal institutions of postwar middle-class democracy.

The social contract established since the Roosevelt years and the institutional mechanisms protecting members of the U.S. manufacturing class (i.e., having provided for significant government influence on the economy, strong trade unions, Social Security and a sustainable minimum wage) are facing systematic disempowerment and dismantling. Ever since the 1980s, the number of unionized jobs providing health and pension insurance cover and allowing ordinary people to buy a house and send their kids to college has declined dramatically.[2] The system of organized labor, thanks to which the manufacturing class had become an integral part of U.S. society with entitlements for participation in the nation's increasing prosperity and wealth, has come under sustained attack from the representatives of a wealthy power elite.

The spectacular decision taken in 2011 by the governor of Wisconsin, Scott Walker, to strip state employees of their collective bargaining power (and hence prospectively of their retirement

---

[1] Hedges, *Empire of Illusion*, 167s.
[2] According to Hedges, *Empire of Illusion*, 168, unionization in the private sector was down from one third in 1974 to 7.8% in 2007. In fact, the rate dropped even further to 7.0% in 2013.

benefits and healthcare entitlements) followed three decades of systematic disempowerment of the institution of unionized labor. After years of massive decline of union power and union membership in the private sector — including the motor industry, where the once mighty United Automobile Workers of America has proved unable to halt the erosion of working standards, wages and pension claims — public services are being targeted as one of the last segments of the working world in which the institutions of organized labor can still hold their ground.

Faced with a massive reduction of real wages and cuts in unemployment benefits and Social Security, middle and lower class Americans are forced to fund increased shares of consumption and access to services like education and health care through mortgages, consumer lending and credit card debt. As a consequence, wide sections of the U.S. middle and manufacturing class have come to live in fear of poverty, excessive indebtedness and social decline.

More and more, the financial and economic elite and its political representatives appear unwilling to maintain a policy of compromise and uphold the levels of social coherence attained in the days of the New Deal. Instead, they vigorously demand the extension of tax cuts for the highest earners and further cutbacks on welfare for the poor. Insisting that those who have proved to be failures must not escape their predicament or be deprived of their natural right to perish, Tea Party activists have called for massive cuts in social spending, i.e., reduced expenditure on healthcare, social housing and public education.

Admittedly, there have been times in U.S. history in which the levels of inequality and social disparity were even higher than today, especially during the Gilded Age in the late 19th century, dominated by corporate magnates, tycoons and vast fortunes, and epitomized by names like Rockefeller and J.P. Morgan. The disconcerting fact about present-day America, however, is the deliberate abandonment and prospective destruction of an already established and accomplished social compromise.

Just as the constitutional compromise (established in 287 B.C. after the end of the Conflict of the Orders), began collapsing in Rome since the mid-second century B.C., there are strong indications that the social contract in America — established in the days of Roosevelt and the New Deal — is being deliberately abandoned and is coming apart in the early years of the 21st century.

The uncompromising attitudes adopted by major sections of the U.S. power elite resemble in structural terms the intransigence and unwillingness to compromise seen among the ruling elites of late republican Rome. The fiercely uncompromising relationship between the *optimates* (defending the privileges of the nobility) and the *populares* (trying to provide for a certain level of social justice and a more equitable distribution of wealth) in the late years of the Roman republic, when the basic constitutional compromise established in 287 B.C. collapsed, finds its counterpart in the increased ideological intensity and bitterness of opposition between Democrats and Republicans and the ferocity with which the Christian Right is fighting the "liberal establishment" and the established institutions of government.

As Rome's political life turned increasingly disruptive and was marked by the mutual vetoing of legislation since the second century B.C., so U.S. budgetary policies have become progressively embittered ever since the extended government shutdowns of the Clinton tenure. Whereas the Europeans once admired the pragmatic spirit of political parties and political life in the U.S., which had the blessing of not being hamstrung by the old, ideological divisions of Europe, things have now almost turned the other way round as the bitterness of bipartisan opposition in the U.S. contrasts with the exhaustion of intellectual fervor and ideological zeal in Europe. The more social and economic pressure is put on the U.S. working and middle class as the central pillar of moderate center-left and center-right politics, the more disruptive, erratic and volatile America's political life appears to be.

In summary, it therefore seems as though the rise to unrivalled superpower status has tended to weaken the *coil* (George Packer) that held together the Americans and, in their time, the ancient Romans.[1] As was already understood in ancient Rome by contemporaries like Poseidonos and Sallust, the lack of serious external enemies sapped the readiness for internal social and political compromise:

---

[1] Obviously, this is an example that, by contrast to what Spengler believed, key historical developments like the loss of social cohesion and the neglect of the superpower's economic basis do allow for causal explanation and not merely represent a consequence of bio-societal ageing and exhaustion.

"The masters of the Mediterranean world thought they could afford (inner) conflict, since they were no longer subject to the discipline imposed by an outside threat."[1] No longer having to fear an outside rival, the power elites of Rome after the Second Punic War and the power elites of the United States after the decline and fall of the Soviet bloc no longer see a need to make concessions to the lesser ranks of society. They feel no compulsion any longer to preserve the bases of national unity, the levels of social concord and domestic cohesion that had been attained over the course of time (and which were deemed indispensable during periods in which the Romans and Americans were still faced with mighty enemies and external rivals such as Carthage, Macedonia, Pyrrhus of Epirus, Nazi Germany or the USSR).[2]

Against this backdrop, however, it comes as a warning from history that the mounting social polarization and disregard of national cohesion (or domestic unity and concord) in ancient Rome eventually undermined the foundations of the republic and upset the internal institutional balance which had once ensured the functioning of government and the settlement of internal, political and social conflict within the constitutional frameworks and limits.

THE ROLE OF ORGANIZED MONEY IN POLITICS [3]

Whereas blue-collar workers and wide sections of the middle class are under pressure from cheap foreign labor and are threatened by high debt and the risk of foreclosure, oligarchic moneyed interests threaten to seize control of Americans politics and public life. Just as politics turned into a battleground for the millionaires and billionaires in late republican Rome in the late second and first century B.C., the political arena in America has become extremely monetized and largely dependent on donations and contributions from a small, wealthy percentage of the population.

---

[1]   Jürgen von Ungern-Sternberg, *The Crisis of the Republic*, in: Flower (ed.), 89-109. 91.

[2]   For example, as pointed out by Monte L. Pearson, an extensive debt reduction scheme passed in 342 B.C. was motivated by troubles and setbacks in the war waged by Rome against a Latin League since 348 B.C. (Pearson, 80s.).

[3]   Along with social inequality and the role of the *publicani*, the increasing role of money in Roman and American politics is also discussed by Pearson, 160-176.

According to estimates, the two main presidential candidates in the 2012 electoral campaign spent more than $1 billion each, for the first time ever. The bulk of these funds was provided by wealthy individuals, families and corporations (especially those in the financial sector, oil and gas companies, insurance, defense corporations and pharmaceutical enterprises). In 2014, a new record of $3.4 billion is estimated to have been spent on the midterm congressional election campaign, and the financial sector alone is estimated to have spent more than $5 billion on political campaigning and lobbying in the period from 2001 to 2010. Further accelerating these trends, the Supreme Court allowed so-called "Super PACs," that is, political campaigning organizations controlled by wealthy individuals and corporations, to raise unlimited funds for the sponsoring of presidential and congressional campaigns starting in 2010. Elsewhere, estimates indicate that a U.S. senator must now raise least $50,000 each day during his 6-year term in office to wage a promising campaign for re-election.

According to George Packer, early 21st century politicians have factually turned into entrepreneurs who depend on special interests, PACs, lobbyists and think tanks rather than on party platforms or apparatuses, civic groups and labor organizations. At the same time, lobbyists author corporate-friendly legislation and press Congress to get it passed, while corporate-controlled media seek to form the minds of commonplace Americans, and corporate leaders make donations to think tanks promoting deregulation and a further crackdown on trade unions, Social Security and the welfare state.[1] As Packer shows, U.S. politics is increasingly controlled by a small elite, i.e., a network of politicians, lobbying firms and corporations in a system of revolving doors between government and the private sector, especially military corporations, finance and oil.[2]

Elected under the sponsorship of billionaire families, corporate donors and special interests, Congress and the government allow the treasury to be looted for the benefit of the financial sector, oil and gas companies and arms corporations, whilst refusing to help the millions of middle class families forced out of their homes because of soaring debt, bank repossession and foreclosure. (The latter hit a peak of 2.8 million cases in 2009 alone and another 2.4 million in 2010

---

[1] Packer, 22.
[2] Packer, 163ss.

— with those affected facing the prospect of having to live in a tent, a trailer or a car, if worst comes to worst). While Social Security is cut back, the quality of public schooling declines and public housing is neglected, billions in taxpayer money have been spent to save banks, insurance companies and other financial sector corporations. This carries echoes indeed of the situation in late republican Rome, where politics became a matter of immensely rich individuals pursuing increasingly personal interests and private agendas without concern for the common good.

More and more, the financial foundations of the state are undermined and the concerns of ordinary Americans are disregarded in a manner strikingly similar to ancient Rome in the late second and early first century B.C., when the senators and wealthy knights started looting the public treasury and closed their eyes to the mounting distress of average Romans (or the plebeian sections of the population). Finally, the recurring attempts to curb the influence of lobbyism and contain the role of organized money in politics tend to come to nothing in the United States just as, in late republican Rome, endeavors to limit the number of participants in election canvassing meals and to curb the spending on electoral banquets failed to stop the practice of vote-buying and end the undue monetary interference in the republic's electoral process.

SOCIO-CULTURAL SEGREGATION

Moreover, we also see rising levels of social and cultural segregation in late republican Rome and present-day America, as both the elites and the lower classes tend to dissociate themselves from the institutional fabrics and essential values of the nation. In the late Roman republic, the social and political elite increasingly segregated itself through the private display of wealth and the lavish furnishing of villas outside the city of Rome, decorated with Greek statues, sculptures and mosaics as symbols of status and class distinction. In the first century B.C., the leading politicians no longer acted as agents of the common good but pursued their own personal agendas as they were eager, in particular, to obtain large military commands allowing them to exploit the natural and financial resources of a province for the sake of private enrichment and personal power accumulation. On the other end of the social spectrum, the urban proletarian masses also cast aside their loyalty to the public institutions and essential values (or republican virtues) of Rome and lost their capacity to actively contribute to the city's political life, seeking instead free meals or grain and amusement at the steadily rising number of triumphal processions, sporting contests and games.

In present-day America, a fundamental disparity of values and lifestyles is arising as well between a wealthy oligarchic elite and broad sections of the lower middle and working class. Increasingly, the elite secludes itself in elite schools, elite universities and gated communities guarded by private security, while publicly accessible education, infrastructure (roads, bridges, urban water systems) and healthcare services decay. The fact that Swiss banks have helped some of their wealthy American clients to exchange passports and renounce U.S. citizenship for tax saving purposes — and, at another level, the projects pursued by influential representatives of the Silicon Valley industry to create artificial floating islands in the Pacific Ocean outside the sovereign claims and regulatory restrictions of the United States — indicate that at least certain sections of America's economic and financial elite are in danger of losing touch with the civic values and constitutional foundations of the nation. Here again, echoes of the late years of the Roman republic can be heard, when the pursuit of one's own personal advantage and widespread disregard for the common good started vitiating the patriotic spirit.

Given the particular way in which the American constitution has been worshipped and venerated throughout the history of the United States, it is a disconcerting fact that leading representatives of the new economic and financial elite not only hold government institutions in contempt as a hostile force, they also show an open disdain for the constitutional system itself. In fact, sections of the new, creative economic and financial elite have begun embracing extreme libertarian views, believing — in the words of Peter Thiel, an influential figure in the Silicon Valley industry — that "the U.S. Constitution is unworkable and has to be scrapped."[1]

However, social cohesion and the bonds holding Americans together, i.e., the set of shared values that once formed the basis of national unity and strength, are not only challenged from the higher societal ranks. On the other end of the social spectrum, parts

---

[1] Thiel as quoted in Packer, 390.

of America's dispossessed manufacturing workforce are in danger of becoming a permanent underclass of chronically unemployed or underemployed working poor and economically useless consumers. As a matter of fact, 47 million U.S. citizens (one in seven Americans) lived on food stamps in 2012, and a new underclass is about to emerge whose members tend to be dependent in a manner strikingly similar to how the Roman proletarians were once dependent on the free supply of grain. Living on income tax credits as they cannot sustain themselves even with a full-time job, parts of the dispossessed working class no longer believe in political participation or the possibility of social advancement through education and personal achievement. For them, the basic American values of industriousness, religion and strong family bonds have begun to ring hollow. Increasingly, these poorer sections of society live in a fundamentally different culture, where families and communities are eroded as overeating, excessive TV consumption and drug abuse are common means of evading reality.

As we shall see below, the impending erosion of the socio-economic, political and cultural foundations of American society is already having a visibly adverse impact in terms of the political climate and the nature of public discourse as well. It remains to be seen whether the United States will manage to find new forms of social balance and equilibrium — and new levels of adherence to its basic civic values — or whether the current social distortions will eventually have sustained repercussions in the nation's political life resembling those once endured by late republican Rome.

The Privatization of War

In America today, the authority of the state is undermined, as it was in late republican Rome, by a comprehensive privatization of government functions and public services from education, hospitals, utilities and infrastructure down to law enforcement, border control, defense and jurisprudence (given the trend to replace regular courts with private arbitration boards). Clearly, these developments are reminiscent of the activities of the *publicani* in the late years of the Roman republic, who took over public functions such as the building of infrastructure, mine operation, and provisioning the army, and they made huge profits out of public contracting just as U.S. corporations like Halliburton are making fortunes today on government-awarded contracts.[1]

In both cases, the frenzy of privatization indicates a structural degradation of the public spirit and detachment from the public weal, as it signals a loss of civic engagement and mounting preference for personal advantage over national interest. Economically, the urge for privatization in late republican Rome as well as in present-day America results, not least, from the need to invest the huge profits accumulated through cheap labor and, in particular, from the massive inflow of capital into Rome and America respectively after the superpower's acquisition of global economic and financial supremacy. In both events, the steady inflow of funds is used by private investors to buy up government-controlled enterprises and public assets (such as stated-owned land in particular in the case of ancient Rome) and take charge of functions previously performed by the government or public institutions.

Within this context, the most striking parallel between late republican Rome and present-day America surely is to be seen in the privatization of defense and defense-related functions. Since the mid-second century B.C., the citizen army and militia system of the early Roman republic was successively replaced with professional troops who no longer owed their loyalty to the institutions of the state but to their respective individual commander. In fact, already the armies of the late second and early first century B.C. were armies not so much of the Roman republic but of individual generals and commanders like Marius or Sulla. In the final years of the republic, the trend towards privatization accelerated and intensified further: the first commander to raise a purely private army at his personal expense and without formal entitlement from the magistrates was Pompey the Great, who thus acted in the capacity of a *privatus cum imperio* in 83 B.C.[2]

Soon afterwards, owners of huge fortunes like Crassus began maintaining their own armies and making their services available to the government on an occasional basis. In this context, military service was no longer about defending the nation and ancestral soil but rather about subjugating foreign peoples and kingdoms and expanding into distant territories for the sake of private enrichment, financial interest and personal fame. As the old republic turned into a "pre-

[1] This parallel is also emphasized by Pearson, p. 169-171.
[2] Ungern-Sternberg, 99.

imperial republic," established *provincias* and detached itself from the original, inherent interests of the nation, the result was widespread unwillingness among the citizens to serve in the Roman army. For the first time, avoidance of the draft became a mass phenomenon in 168 B.C., prior to the preventive Third Macedonian War, and then again in 151 B.C. during a campaign for the submission of rebellions in Spain, wars which were no longer fought for national survival and interest but rather for the extension of global supremacy and the subjugation of foreign nations.

As the policies of the republic became disconnected from the ancestral soil (and territory) and detached from national interest, it was only logical that the traditional concept of a citizen army was successively dismissed, military service lost its appeal to the artisans and peasants, and the Roman army could no longer draw on its traditional reservoir, the citizen-farmer-soldier.

Instead, troop recruiters began resorting to mercenaries and professional soldiers, many of whom were members of the urban proletarian mass or were aliens from Greece, Africa, Minor Asia and other regions recently subjected to Roman dominion and control. Furnished with long-term contracts, the new soldiers were entirely dependent on their generals or commanders, who they hoped would provide them with a piece of land so they could make a living after their army service careers. Before long, the soldiers' personal commitment to the commander outweighed any sense of loyalty to the Roman nation, constitution and state. In the end, the personally committed soldiers helped their commanders brush aside the institutions of the republic as they staged a succession of "marches on Rome" under the commanderships of Marius, Sulla, Pompey and finally Julius Caesar.

In present-day America, we are likewise seeing extensive privatization not only of public services like education, hospitals, utilities and law enforcement but also of the armed forces sector, as a rising share of military functions are turned over to private service providers. Especially during the wars on Afghanistan and Iraq, substantial scopes of U.S. military activity were outsourced to defense contractors and mercenary corporations like Academi (formerly known as Blackwater), Military Professional Resources Inc. (MPRI), Steele Foundation, Harris Corporation or Kellogg, Brown and Root (i.e., KBR, a former subsidiary of Halliburton). Especially during the occupation of Iraq, the Bush administration deployed a shadow army of heavily armed mercenary forces essentially operating under impunity from U.S. criminal prosecution.

By the end of Donald Rumsfeld's tenure, the number of private contractor personnel on the ground in Iraq had increased to 100,000 — an almost 1:1 ratio with regular U.S. troops.[1] As a matter of fact, the Blackwater forces not only provided training services and logistical support, they also operated prisons and guarded ammunition depots, having their own armored vehicles, helicopter gunships, parachuting units and satellite-guided weapons. On a number of occasions, regular U.S. marines were given firing orders by Blackwater staff, such as in Najaf in 2004, when hundreds of Iraqi casualties resulted from the lifting of a siege of the local U.S. headquarters.[2] Operating under impunity, outside public oversight and jurisdiction, the private defense contractors were explicitly not subject to the rules and limitations governing the conduct of regular U.S. army personnel.

As Jeremy Scahill has shown, Blackwater forces were disconcertingly immunized from public prosecution and civil litigation. They were not held accountable for firing at crowds and civilian vehicles or for other incidents, the bloodiest of which was the punitive pacification mission carried out on the city of Fallujah in 2004. Once again, this is all remarkably similar to the *pre-imperial* military contingents operating for essentially private purposes and on essentially private agendas in the name of the Roman republic during the late second and first century B.C. Like modern private defense contractors in the United States, the Roman army contingents ended up dissociating themselves from the basic interests of the nation and serving essentially private financial and political interests. They could no longer be held accountable by the authorities and institutions of the Roman state (much to the disapproval of many long-standing senators) for atrocities committed in Spain, Gaul and other insurrectional regions.

In late republican Rome, rising proportions of the troops consisted of foreigners, and Roman legionaries were drawn from all parts of the ancient world (as they were promised Roman citizenship and old-age provisions after a certain number of service years). Similarly, significant percentages of the private defense contractor personnel

---

[1] Scahill, XVII.
[2] Scahill, 129.

deployed on behalf of the United States around the world actually come from foreign countries like the Philippines, Chile, Colombia, Honduras, El Salvador, Peru, Fiji or Nepal. In fact, many of the mercenary soldiers, and also many of the regular U.S. army staff that died in action in Afghanistan or Iraq, were not U.S. citizens proper but "green card soldiers," i.e., foreign nationals primarily from South and Central America, Southeast Asia and Eastern Europe, who had been promised American citizenship in exchange for several years of military service.

There is much to suggest that in present-day America, just as in late republican Rome, the disconnection of a hegemony-aspiring, *pre-imperial* republic from the original concerns and innate interests of the nation is triggering a shift of military recruitment. Instead of conscripts, we see more and more professional, voluntary soldiers and private army contingents, drawn no longer from national but from international sources. In both cases, the citizens themselves become increasingly reluctant to risk their lives and shed their blood for causes which they perceive as far removed (such as putting down rebellions in places like ancient Spain and modern Iraq).

As Rome's original militia system, drawing on a pool of regularly demobilizing farmers, could not be maintained anymore in view of the city's rise to global hegemony and predominance, the increasingly hegemonic and *pre-imperial* policies pursued by the United States are causing natural reluctance among many American citizens to serve in the armed forces in ever-more distant and hence unpopular wars. As a consequence, the draft has been abolished, and the U.S. army increasingly resorts to using aliens and private defense resources.

As for the private defense contractors in America, their disconnection from the basic interests of the nation is also reflected in the fact that they now offer their services across the world, no longer to the U.S. alone, and that they serve not only national authorities but also private companies, banks and wealthy individuals. They push for internationalization and aspire to establish themselves as independent, global military players offering services like elite force training, counter-terrorism and counter-insurgency to wealthy governments and corporations, especially in Africa and the Middle East. As for Blackwater, Jeremy Scahill has described the company as hoping to take peace-making and peacekeeping "business," for instance in Sudan or Haiti, away from international organizations like the UN, NATO or the African and European Unions.[1]

Disconcertingly, a leading Halliburton manager has observed that "the more aggressively the U.S. expands its military reach, the better [it is] for Halliburton's business."[2] Statements like this are indications of a prospective threat that private interests may, at some point, drag the United States into policies of aggrandizement, pursuit of hegemony and pre-imperial expansion in a manner similar to late republican Rome — where powerful individuals, tax collectors and public contracting companies pushed for expansion and war as a means of private enrichment, personal fame and political power accumulation. (In the late republican years, leading Roman politicians squeezed huge amounts of money out of the provinces and client kingdoms to fund their electoral campaigns and win the votes of ordinary Romans by providing free bread, meals, games and prestigious construction projects.[3])

In particular, people like Crassus and Caesar started wars of conquest for the sake of personal interest and private profit (while Crassus died in his self-instigated campaign against the Parthians, Caesar's strategy finally paid off — on the back of one million Gauls who died in Rome's colonial campaign of subjugation).[4] Judging by historical analogy, there is a looming threat that, just as in ancient Rome, privatized military power may entice America into pursuing increasingly aggressive aims and expansionary objectives and striving for an excessive enlargement of its hegemonic (power–political) reach.

In addition, there are disquieting indications already today that unaccountable pre-imperial practices — i.e., unlimited executive force, the treatment of enemy combatants without respect for constitutional constraints and international law (such as the Geneva Convention) and the use of private military power abroad — have begun migrating back to the center and menacing the basic values of the American republic itself.

Under the USA Patriot Act, constitutional liberties have been limited and extensive profiles have been created — of millions of American citizens, not only of enemy combatants — through data

---

[1] Scahill, 347-349.
[2] Scahill, XVI.
[3] Badian, 79ss.
[4] Badian, 89.

mining, wire-tapping and eavesdropping without legal oversight and the previously required court-approved warrants.

With a view to widening government reach, the Bush administration directed lawyers in the Departments of Justice and Defense in the summer of 2002 to review the Posse Comitatus Act and other related laws designed to restrict the participation of the U.S. military in domestic law enforcement and intelligence gathering on citizens in the United States without judicial oversight and authorization.[1] As Chalmers Johnson has stated, the Bush administration "arrogated to itself the power to judge whether an American citizen is part of a terrorist organization and could therefore be stripped of all constitutional rights."[2]

The repercussion of extra-constitutional practices and "imperialist" techniques on the United States itself — thus far reserved for "enemies" in embattled fringe regions — became obvious especially in 2004, when the Supreme Court ruled that police may enter homes of American citizens without knocking,[3] and in the idea of using fighter drones over American territory after their successful deployment in Pakistan, Afghanistan and Iraq. In March 2013, Attorney General Eric Holder told an interviewer that, technically and in particular circumstances, the U.S. administration would be entitled to use fighter drones to kill American citizens on American soil, as the president was permitted to authorize the assassination of U.S. citizens deemed complicit in terror.

The most disquieting incident, however — and, as Scahill noted, a "dangerous precedent that could undermine U.S. democracy"[4] — was that, after Hurricane Katrina hit New Orleans on 29 August 2005, hundreds of heavily armed Blackwater mercenaries, some fresh from Iraq, were deployed in the disaster zone. Dressed in full battle gear with khaki uniforms, wraparound sunglasses, and beige military boots, with automatic assault guns and Blackwater IDs on their arms, they patrolled the streets in SUVs with tinted windows and Blackwater logos, commissioned to support the fight against criminals and looters.[5]

---

[1] Johnson, *Sorrows of Empire*, 121.
[2] Johnson, *Sorrows of Empire*, 293.
[3] Murphy, 40.
[4] Scahill, 334.
[5] Scahill, 323-325.

In fact, the Blackwater troops were authorized to carry loaded weapons, make arrests and even use lethal force. In security industry circles, New Orleans and the surrounding disaster area were explicitly referred to as "Baghdad on the Bayou ... as if the Tigris — rather than the Mississippi — had flooded the city."[1]

Hired by the Department of Homeland Security, the private contractor forces were explicitly not subject to the usual constitutional limitations. In addition, Scahill has also reported the Blackwater Corporation as seeking to take over decisive sections of domestic security, namely the deployment of armed private patrols to control immigration on the southern border and the outsourcing of border security to the private sector.[2]

Looking at the fate of ancient Rome in the first century B.C., the deployment of Blackwater troops on U.S. soil is a warning sign, reminding us that private armies originally operating on the fringes of a hegemonic, pre-imperial republic might one day wish to become a factor of power in national politics. Forms of private, unaccountable and unlimited executive force threaten to gain ground in America itself and establish themselves as rivals and alternatives to the limited, lawful executive practices of accountable, constitutional institutions.

Already in the immediate aftermath of Hurricane Katrina, Michael Ratner, president of the *Center for Constitutional Rights*, suggested that "here at home in the United States, controlling an angry, abused population with a police force bound to obey the Constitution can be difficult — private forces can solve this 'problem'."[3] As it did in the late years of the Roman republic, the pursuance of "pre-imperial" policies abroad threatens to result in a transfer of powers from citizen-controlled institutions to private military structures, which, from a certain point onwards, may no longer be willing to accept the rules and restrictions of national constitutional law.

As we saw above, it has always been a great concern among true and devoted republicans that mercenary armies and private military forces operating on the fringes of a hegemony-aspiring republic could finally turn on their host and help undermine the institutional foundations of constitutional liberty and government. In this context, it is certainly worth mentioning that the owners of the Blackwater

---

[1] Scahill, 329s.
[2] Scahill, 335.
[3] Scahill, XXIV.

Corporation, the Prince family, have been committed enduringly to right wing, conservative Christian causes. Together with other companies of the private security and military contracting sector, Blackwater paid large amounts of money to ensure that Republicans won a majority in Congress, enhancing the industry's prospects of immediate access to the political decision-makers. According to Scahill, Blackwater CEO Erik Prince served "as a major bankroller not only of President Bush's campaigns but of broader Christian-right agendas."[1]

During the years of the Clinton administration, the Prince family and other influential owners of private defense corporations played an active part in conservative circles, in the eyes of which the Clinton administration was an antireligious, faith-suppressing regime, whose moral illegitimacy might even justify the idea of resistance, for which the Christians sections of society were advised to prepare.[2]

In summary, the prerogative to operate outside the law and governmental authority within the United States and the urge of the private military contractor industry to usurp original government functions constitute a danger that, one day, privatized defense and unaccountable military practice might pose a threat to the constitutional foundations of the American republic, as they once did in late republican Rome. The looming threat is that the great respect for the law and legal procedures — by which ancient Rome and modern America have stood out and distinguished themselves from others — may, at some point in the future, fall victim to unaccountable practices which are nourished by omnipotence abroad and finally migrate back to the heart and center itself.

CIVIC DISCONNECTION AND THE RISE OF IRRATIONAL BELIEF

In socio-cultural terms, a characteristic shared by late republican Rome and present-day America is the trend toward social atomization and civic disconnection. In the case of ancient Rome, the urban masses of the first century B.C. were no longer capable of acting in concert and bringing their interests to bear collectively as a powerful, institutionalized political factor like the traditional plebs had been in the third and early second century B.C. Instead, a conglomeration of

---

[1]   Scahill, XIX.
[2]   Scahill, 30s.

progressively disconnected individuals arose who no longer sought a practical remedy to their economic misery and social plight but showed a growing inclination to mythical thought and irrational belief.

Whereas anti-rational thought had still been disapproved, and prominent astrologers had still been expelled from the city of Rome in 139 B.C., increasing sections of the urban populace in the first century B.C. started believing in magic, miracles and fortune telling. While Rome was still the epitome of reason and rational practice, seen as the capital of sobriety withstanding the surge of anti-rationalist belief emanating from the Hellenistic east in the second century B.C., the late Roman republic saw ever more people subscribe to witchcraft, astrology, dream reading, fortune telling, prophecy and other forms of mysticist and occultist thought.

As loyalty to the institutions of the state declined and the once strong identification with the political community faltered, many Romans abandoned the traditional, state-controlled national religion in favor of the mystery cults and occultist practices from Hellenistic and oriental sources. No longer committed to the old municipal gods, which had always been tied to particular places and institutions of the Roman state, more and more Romans of the late second and first century B.C. sought for individual salvation and consolation, which also came to be reflected in the massive growth of private religious associations.

Instead of traditional mediation via the official city cults, the municipal temples, the pontifex, the pater familias or the Vestal Virgins, religion now tended to be practiced on an essentially personal basis, as individual religiousness and the pursuit of a personal relationship with the divinity prevailed over the ancestral cults of the city, the house and the fields (where the entire family or *res publica* had made contact with the gods through the pater familias and the state-appointed priests). Practical reason was not only challenged in the area of religion, however, but also in terms of philosophy, where skepticism was on the rise, and skeptic philosophers taught their audiences that man could not trust his senses, that human knowledge was questionable in principle and that no safe ground existed to distinguish between falsehood and truth, reality and deceit.

In the final analysis, the massive rise of irrational belief in late republican Rome resulted intrinsically from a general trend to social disconnection and political disempowerment. As a matter of fact, this was a time when active commitment to the res publica declined, involvement in the political institutions faltered and many people sought to avoid participating in the heavily manipulated elections. Instead, a society of progressively disconnected individuals arose, in which traditional social and political bonds disintegrated and collapsed. Not least, the trade and neighborhood associations (or collegia), which the old plebs had used to employ as a means of communication and political mobilization, and through which it had asserted itself as a forceful, independent political actor, were systematically disempowered after their violent suppression during Sulla's dictatorship in 82–79 B.C.

The new society of isolated (solipsistic) individuals, however, no longer provided the room to take communicative political action, exchange views with one's fellow citizens and develop the *sensus communis* which, as Aristotle had already pointed out, is an indispensable prerequisite for the proper perception of reality. As Hannah Arendt showed in *The Human Condition*, maintenance of the *sensus communis* essentially requires involvement in political institutions and civic associations, i.e., social ties with one's fellow citizens that allow the individual to judge and check his opinions against those of his peers.

Explicitly, Arendt pointed out that "the presence of others who see what we see and hear what we hear assures us of the reality of the world."[1] If the common world falls apart, however, and everybody is "imprisoned in the subjectivity of his own singular experience,"[2] people are bound to lose their capacity to perceive the reality of the outside world: "The only character of the world by which to gauge its reality is its being common to us all ... It is by virtue of common sense that the other sense perceptions are known to disclose reality and are not merely felt as irritations of our nerves or resistance sensations of our bodies. A noticeable decrease in common sense in any given community and a noticeable increase in superstition and gullibility are therefore almost infallible signs of alienation from the world."[3]

---

[1] Arendt, *The Human Condition*, 50.
[2] Arendt, *The Human Condition*, 58.
[3] Arendt, *The Human Condition*, 208s.

Against this backdrop, however, it was a consequence of social disintegration, civic atomization and the political disempowerment of ordinary citizens that people in late republican Rome became increasingly dissociated from reality, stopped trusting their senses and began subscribing to forces of magical thought and irrational belief. What had happened many years before in the Hellenistic world, when allegiance to the nation and belief in the authority of the body politic had faltered since the fourth and third century B.C., now began afflicting Rome itself.

In the Hellenistic context, rational thought had declined and the mysteries of Isis, Osiris, Cybele and Serapis (along with other forms of mythicist and occultist belief and the philosophy of skepticism as the guiding school of thought) had ascended in the same measure in which the authority of the polis and people's involvement in the institutions (or political life) of the city-state had diminished since the late fourth century B.C.[1] — and hence the civic ties forming prerequisites of the sensus communis and the confidence to trust one's own senses had broken down. In those days, though, the wave of mythical thought, irrational belief, astrology and fortune-telling emanating from the Hellenistic east was still met with fierce resistance and strong rejection in Rome itself, which stubbornly maintained itself as a stronghold of rationality and reason.

Since the second century B.C., however, when the citizens of Rome became increasingly isolated from each other and alienated from the city's institutional and political life, rationality was progressively dismissed and magical thought successively advanced. Instead of adherence to the old municipal cults and republican religions, the flagellant, self-mutilating followers of Cybele now started marching the streets, as broad sectors of the urban populace began embracing syncretistic religions of Phrygian, Syrian and Egyptian origin or fell victim to charlatans or pretended prophets, and private religious communities established themselves on the sacred places of the old municipal cults — despite the fact that, for instance, the temple of Isis alone was closed down four times by the municipal authorities between 59–48 B.C. and restrictions were imposed by the magistrates on the cult of the magna mater, which limited the activities of the Galli, the Phrygian eunuch priests, to particular days.[2]

---

[1] Walbank, 223.
[2] Orlin, 63.

Yet, even though priests were arrested, gatherings prohibited and shrines dismantled, the state was unable to halt the steady rise of religious communities and cultic practices outside the city's traditional politico-religious framework. In addition, the surge of skeptic philosophy in Rome in the years of the late republic (like in the heyday of postclassical, Hellenistic Greece) likewise suggests that many Romans were no longer ready to trust their senses in an atmosphere where isolation was on the rise and people felt out of touch with national institutions and their fellow-citizens. Occult mysteries, oriental religion, superstition and astrology advanced apace as identification with the fabrics of the constitution and active involvement in the city's public life declined especially among the lower and middle classes. The populace and urban proletarian mass, by which the traditional society of artisans and peasants had progressively been replaced since the start of the second century B.C., were no longer tied to the soil of the land or ancestral property (from which many of them had been expelled), no longer involved in the city's political life and hence no longer rooted in matters of the world to the extent required for developing a sound sense of objectivity and proper perception of reality.

The civic atomization and social disconnection that resulted from the loss of social cohesion and collective political organization gave rise to a mental and intellectual environment in which unreason and mythical thought could flourish, as common sense was undermined and people turned from the perception of reality to irrational hopes and beliefs. As a general fact, this was no longer a world shaped by man through common political action, a worldly context of long-lasting property and political organization, but of civic disconnection and political disintegration nurturing apocalyptic thought and the unconditional subjection of man to universal divine force.

In a structurally similar manner, Chris Hedges has described early 21st-century America as an "empire of illusion" where objectivity is dismissed in favor of magical thought, and increased sections of society are running out of touch with reality. Hedges refers to a culture of spectacle and illusion, media images and corporate-created simulacra, in which people seek escape from reality and tend to embrace myths "on which millions can hang their fears and hopes."[1]

---

[1] Hedges, *Empire of Illusion*, 16.

Whereas the United States was still the epitome of common sense and reason when large parts of Europe fell victim to ideological fanaticism in the 1930s, religious fanaticism and fictitious belief now threaten to jeopardize rationality as substantial sections of American society no longer have confidence in science and the power of rational argumentation. Rather than using practical and constructive means to improve the lives of ordinary, middle and working class Americans, reactions to the widespread fear of social decline include the rejection of the theory of evolution and scientific education, the denial of man-made global warming, the subscription to apocalyptic thought and the search for universal conspiracy.

The religious right in America has not only become increasingly politicized and seen a significant rise in the number of activists and followers, it has also adopted substantially more extreme and aggressive views over the last 30 years. As Joe Bageant has pointed out in *Deer Hunting with Jesus*, present-day American society is marked by widespread fictional belief and "millions of fundamentalists producing their own mind movies of American reality, in which the secretary general of the United Nations is the Antichrist and the 'Clinton crime family' deals in cocaine..."[1] Like in the late years of the Roman republic, charismatic leaders and movements have emerged, which turn their backs on the reality of the world and seek deliverance in unreason.

Referring to the surge of fundamentalist zeal and end-times theology, Bageant claimed "that millions of Americans are under the spell of an extraordinarily dangerous mass psychosis,"[2] especially as far as socially hard pressed working and lower class whites are concerned — thus forming the basis of an intellectual environment in which questions like whether Obama is the Antichrist or whether the United Nations is a tool of Evil have become subjects of serious debate.[3] Other apocalyptic visions shared by significant sections of the Christian fundamentalist community include the Christian Zionist notion that Israel should be encouraged to expand into ever more *holy territory*, as Israel (allegedly according to the Bible) must first encompass all the biblical lands before the apocalyptic destruction of the rebuilt Temple of Jerusalem and the Second Coming of Christ

---

[1] Bageant, *Deer Hunting with Jesus. Dispatches from America's Class War*, New York 2007, 184.
[2] Bageant, 190.
[3] Bageant, 160ss.

can occur, and that nuclear war in the Middle East might actually accelerate the awaited descent of the Lord.[1]

In the same context, Bageant also refers to the increasingly popular idea of the Rapture, when all Christians, dead and alive, will be bodily taken up to Heaven before the ultimate devastation of the earth begins. In fact, extreme fundamentalists have argued that laws and regulations protecting the environment could actually be scrapped, as protection of the earth no longer makes sense, given the imminent occurrence of the Rapture or other apocalyptic events.

Especially in the poor and rural areas of the South and Midwest, a war against reason seems to be underway. Radio commentators and TV preachers hammer paranoia-inducing ideas into the heads of their viewers and listeners, indicating that an all-embracing conspiracy — including government, the liberal establishment and mainstream education — is in progress to eradicate all traces of Christianity from U.S. soil and merge the United States into a socialist "world state."[2]

The inclination to seek deliverance in unreason in contemporary America traces back to rising levels of individualization, civic atomization and social disconnection, once again paralleling developments in the late years of the Roman republic. As a consequence of extensive deregulation, flexibilization and the steady decline of organizations like trade unions (which had once ensured social cohesion, furnished civic ties and provided room for rational argumentation), wide sections of the present-day American population have become socially exposed, economically unsettled and intellectually insecure.

Stripped of lasting social ties and means of collective organization, individuals find themselves steeped in an essentially narcissistic culture of competitive individualism, in which they are required to find inner strength in self-optimization and rely exclusively on themselves as far as economic survival and social status are concerned.[3] "Alone on a landscape without solid structures," George Packer concludes, "Americans have to improvise their own destinies and plot their own stories of success and salvation."[4] When narrating the story of an immigrant woman running a Comfort Inn in Pasco

---

[1] Bageant, 160ss.
[2] Hedges, *Empire of Illusion*, 175.
[3] Chris Hedges, *Death of the Liberal Class*, New York 2010, 11.
[4] Packer, 4.

County, Florida, with help from members of her family, Packer notes in a very telling phrase that she "was not a native American (i.e., not born in the U.S.), which is to say, she was not alone."[1]

Packer illustrates the radical isolation in which the inhabitants of American suburbia with its single-family homes have come to live. Among other incidents, he shows how a wave of resistance to the projected construction of a light railway system in Tampa, Florida, was motivated by widespread concern that such a system would force people to meet and come in contact with each other. From the objectors' perspective, light rail threatened to create a "society in which people were forced to share public services with strangers ... Rail was a threat to the lifestyle of New Tampa... In New Tampa, you drove to the supermarket once a week" and otherwise avoided meeting or having contact with your fellow citizens.[2] Obviously, the very idea of a light rail system was deemed a threat to the *society of individuals*, which has become the guiding principle of social organization in late 20th and early 21st century America — requiring everybody to behave as an entrepreneur and believe only and exclusively in the power of the self.

In fact, established institutions like trade unions, public schools or universities are not the only structures facing erosion in present-day America. The very edifice of the community, i.e., places where people can meet and communicate — in small churches, pubs, town centers or shops — is being replaced with the highly anonymous world of Wal-mart stores, mega churches and malls. Like it did in late republican Rome, a society of progressively isolated individuals is emerging, people who are out of touch with their fellow citizens and who lose the very capacity of collective political action, social cooperation and civic organization. Deprived of the civic bonds and common institutions providing room (or a framework) for rational argumentation, substantial sections of American society now seek escape from reality and have become susceptible to fundamentalist promises of security and truth.

From a strictly economic perspective, the post-2008 financial crisis has often been compared to the Great Depression of the 1930s. By contrast to the 1930s, however, which were a time of massive working class activism, political struggle, progressive journalism

---

[1] Packer, 276.
[2] Packer, 311.

and farmer militancy, those affected by the post-2008 financial crisis hardly showed any comparable sense of solidarity or collective resistance. Unlike in the years of the Great Depression, there is now a striking lack of public struggle aimed at finding practical ways to improve ordinary people's lives and productive solutions to social exposure and financial plight.

In fact, the acts of resistance from labor unions, community groups or independent media which might have been expected in response to the mounting pressure weighing on America's middle and manufacturing class, have not taken place. Instead, it looks as though a society of individuals is emerging who are so isolated and disconnected from each other that the very capacity of taking productive collective action and seeking practical solutions for the improvement of societal conditions is being lost. The wave of progressive activism, social agitation and radical journalism seen at the beginning of the 20th century and during the Great Depression seems to have no substantial counterpart in the early years of the 21st century. In present-day American society, where people have been trained to consider themselves exclusively as individuals modeling their personal lives on a consumer and celebrity culture, it seems as though the social and cultural foundations of productive political resistance have disappeared.

In an age dominated by the "cult of the self,"[1] we seem to be lacking even the preconditions for developing the collective consciousness and sense of togetherness required for the rational pursuance of interests and productive endeavors to improve the lives of ordinary people. Indeed, the dominant reaction to the post-2008 financial crisis has not been joint political action by those suffering from the consequences of the crisis but rather the fierce insistence on "individual responsibility" even among the sectors of society who lack the means to fulfill such a responsibility, as they struggle with near-poverty and live from paycheck to paycheck. Doggedly rejecting any vision or notion of solidarity, Tea Party activists have insisted that losers must not be helped and that ordinary people should be forced to leave their homes rather than curtailing the freedom of the financial sector or providing government aid to struggling homeowners.

---

[1] Hedges,124.

Though it seems irrational, even those most severely affected by the crisis and the decline of the manufacturing sector show a firm distaste for trade unions and government in general, fiercely committing themselves to the principle of "everybody for himself."[1]

In conclusion, the degradation of blue-collar workers, the mounting social pressure and the rising levels of isolation and distress among the middle and the lower class in 21st-century America fail to generate a productive political struggle in response but rather a search for deliverance in unreason.[2] The intrinsic relationship once described by Hannah Arendt between social disconnection, civic disintegration and collapsing political bonds on the one hand and a general inclination to irrationality and fictitious (or mythical) belief on the other seems to have become a virulent force as well in early 21st century America. As Joe Bageant pointed out in *Deer Hunting with Jesus*, the disintegration of the working world — with declining opportunities for regular employment and swelling ranks of working poor — has produced a general destabilization of living conditions and widespread fears of social decline.

The rising cost of healthcare, the dismantling of workers' rights, the cuts in university scholarships for the middle class and the shortage of affordable housing have left many people struggling with medical bills, home loans and the cost of their children's college education amid a general sentiment of fear, uncertainty and concern. With social disconnection and political disempowerment progressing, the coil of beliefs and expectations that used to hold Americans together and provide a framework of civic interaction and rational argumentation among the citizens increasingly threatens to disintegrate. "American democracy is beset by a sense of crisis. Seismic shifts during a single generation have created a country of winners and losers, driving the political system to the verge of breakdown and setting citizens adrift," George Packer has stated and concluded in *The Unwinding*. According to Packer, Americans are faced with a looming collapse of the social contract and the civic mechanisms protecting ordinary people, as the structures, norms and institutions established since the historical compromise of the *Roosevelt Republic* crumble and begin to decay.[3]

---

[1] Packer, 339ss.
[2] Hedges, *Death of the Liberal Class*, 23.
[3] Packer, 3.

As Thomas Frank has demonstrated in *Pity the Billionaire, The Hard Times Swindle and the Unlikely Comeback of the Right*, the new political movements having emerged on the political right in early 21st century America tend to consist of individuals who refuse to have their view of the world disturbed by arguments, experiences and facts, "protect themselves against the shock of recognition and do not trust the evidence of their senses."[1] Relevant parts of present-day American society no longer seem to have a common civic framework through which to exchange political views and ideas, interact as citizens, take joint political action and develop the essentially "common" sense which is required to perceive reality and come to terms with the world by practical and constructive means.

Many dispossessed and disempowered individuals tend to hang their lives and hopes on illusions and myths, rather than on rational argumentation and joint political action. Thrown back on himself, the individual no longer trusts his senses, falls out of touch with reality and tends to indulge in a world of fantasies, illusions and dreams. No longer trying to practically improve their lives by reasonable political means, many members of the neglected and fearful working and middle class embrace fictitious belief, become susceptible to demagogues and seek relief in detachment from reality. People seeing themselves ever more marginalized economically and socially, and cut off from the perspective of joint civic action, become receptive to conspiracy theory, tend to believe in imaginary threats, and plunge themselves "into the arms of demagogues and charlatans" offering security and relief through miracles and magic.[2]

As once described by Hannah Arendt, it seems as though the rising levels of social disconnection, civic atomization and isolation from one's fellow citizens are about to entice people in 21st century America as well into taking refuge to fictitious worlds and subscribing to irrational thoughts and beliefs.

When Greece and Europe fell victim to a wave of occultist belief and irrational thought in the third century B.C. and early 20th century A.D., respectively, America and Rome still asserted themselves as the bulwarks of rationality and strongholds of reason. As we saw above, people in ancient Greece abandoned the former spirit of rationality

---

[1] Thomas Frank, *Pity the Billionaire. The Hard-Times Swindle and the Unlikely Comeback of the Right*, New York 2012, 157.
[2] Hedges, *Empire of Illusion*, 183.

and embraced the mysteries of Isis and Osiris, Cybele and Serapis, or started believing in miracles, astrology and wonder-healing at a time when the traditional bodies politic collapsed and citizens were out of touch with the inherited political frameworks and institutions of the city-state, immersed in a new culture shaped by individualism and civic isolation (as the municipal spirit declined and the once all-embracing relationship between the city-state and the citizen faltered). In early 20th-century Europe, people likewise subscribed to occultist visions and irrational ideologies in a situation where the legitimacy of national political frameworks was challenged and the pertinence of national political institutions was called into question in the age of imperialism. For Europe, especially the 1920s and 30s were a time characterized, no less than the early 4th and early 3rd century in Hellenistic Greece, by collapsing state institutions, coups d'état, refugees and expellees, while civic atomization and social disconnection began to set in ever since the early 20th century and the devastations caused by World War I.

In fact, both the occultist visions of Hellenistic Greece and the fateful ideologies of 20th-century Europe were marked by what Hannah Arendt has referred to as a sense of radical *worldlessness*. In Hellenistic Greece, the mystery cults required the faithful to emulate the death of the god and sense the experience of death as salvation from the constraints of the human being's worldly existence. At the same time, postclassical philosophy advised the individual not to cling to his external existence and outside entities, seek abstention from matters of the world in introspection, consider his earthly existence only as a brief and sorrowful migration through a world of alienation and welcome death as liberation of the soul from the prison of bodily, material existence (or a step towards eternal tranquility). In Europe during the first half of the 20th century, the ideological forces of Fascism, Nazism and early Communism likewise harbored a fascination with death and longed for apocalyptic disaster. In both cases, the adherents of radical wordlessness endorsed a policy of self-denial and disregard of worldly reality, interests and experiences, as they were driven by a life-negating impetus to inflict and suffer death.

Yet in the days when Greeks and Europeans readily succumbed to unreason, America and Rome respectively had still asserted themselves as sanctuaries of rationality which eventually assumed the cumbersome task of reorganizing the politically torn and hapless worlds of Europe and Greece. In those days, when the Romans still opposed the mystery cults and occultist ideas from the Hellenistic east (as reflected in the closure of temples, the prohibition of cults and the expulsion of priests), the rational organization of the Roman society and state had stood in marked contrast with the deplorable state of affairs in the Hellenistic world, shaken as it was (especially in the fourth and third century B.C.) by proscriptions, revolutions, expropriations, tyrannies and coups d'état, with vast numbers of refugees and expellees, as traditional political standards collapsed, the sophists preached the principle of might makes right, and conventional moral, political and military rules of conduct were no longer observed.

In modern history, the United States assumed the similarly cumbersome task of bringing Europe back to its senses after two world wars, thus putting an end to the devastating rule of nationalist aggression, racial hubris and ideological delusion. As it turned out, only the United States had the capacity and potential to replace the era of boundless, uncontrolled violence which had haunted Europe since World War I with a new tenable, lasting and productive political order after 1945.

As we have seen, however, the inclination to unreason, irrational thought and apocalyptic belief also rose in Rome itself a few centuries later when social cohesion eroded and the institutions of the republic plunged into a finally lethal crisis. At the start of the 21st century, it looks as though the United States can no longer be regarded, either, as the imperturbably safe haven of rationality and that the inner disintegration of American society is taking its toll as well on the rational and pragmatic spirit of America. As in late republican Rome, the degradation of civic ties, the decline of the productive sector, the economic superfluity of many members of the former middle and working class, and the progressing levels of disconnection and isolation among the citizens have created a situation in America where many people seek escape from (external) reality and readily embrace fictitious hopes and beliefs. Haunted by despair and the fear of social decline, they tend to throw themselves into the arms of demagogy, irrationality, apocalyptic vision and pretended magic.

Against this backdrop, the question of whether America will manage to develop new forms of socio-economic cohesion and political equilibrium will be of vital importance as well for the future of its public discourse and political life. It therefore remains to be seen whether the United States will be able to restore the indispensable levels of social cohesion and coil — and hence help to bring those sections of society back to their senses, which have come to develop an inclination to unreason and long for fictitious escape from the harshness and constraints of reality through mythical thought, apocalyptic vision and irrational belief.

In the final analysis, early warning signs have become apparent (including social polarization and segregation, the role of organized money in politics, the increasing bitterness of political conflict and debate, the decline of the nation's productive basis and its transformation into an *empire of consumption*, the privatization of warfare and defense, the new intransigence in foreign policy terms, the disregard of constitutional restraints, the rising levels of civic atomization and the increasing role of irrational, apocalyptic thought in the nation's public discourse and political life), which provide indication that the United States may be about to embark on a course resembling the (pre-imperial) course of Rome in the early years of the late republic.

It remains to be seen whether the United States is indeed so *exceptional* as to withstand the fate of all the universal powers in the history of mankind — or if Spengler was right in claiming that the history of the West (embodied in U.S. world supremacy, which he already foresaw as the ultimate stage of occidental history) will finally endure its inescapable destiny and follow the fateful trajectory of all the universal powers and high cultural formations ever having existed in the course of human history. Will America manage to uphold its republican principles and values – or will charismatic (Caesarean) leaders with authoritarian inclinations begin to emerge, who present themselves as redeemers, offer simple solutions, promise to close the rift within the American nation, and appeal to all sections of society from entrepreneurs and business people down to the pressurized lower and working class?

Finally, an important hint for the prospective future of the West may well lie in the rising intellectual relevance of a softer, cultural version of Marxism. Increasingly popular and intellectually predominant in Western societies, this pattern of thought has been promoting the deconstruction not so much of class, but of nation, gender and race.

As traditional national, racial and sexual identities are cast aside, the individual is supposed to turn into a human being as such, per se and in abstracto. No longer having to fulfill traditional roles and obligations as a member of a nation or family, the individual is supposed to progress (and be released) into absolute subjective freedom. Facing one and the same civilization extending across the world (a globalized economy with the same language and culture), it is able to live, work and feel at home anywhere in the world, as the rights of a citizen are replaced with universal human rights. At the same time, the underlying hope is that, in a world without nations and borders, in which human beings overcome the old divides and are merged prospectively into one consistent uni-race, any reason for war or hatred will be eliminated and eternal peace, harmony and concord will prevail.

There is, however, a dialectic relationship between absolute freedom and absolute control (or absolute subjection). As intermediary entities and bonds (such as the home, the family or the nation) disintegrate, leaving the individual with no place to seek shelter and orientation and no place to which he might withdraw, the individual becomes directly exposed to a global, omnipotent structure of power. In a world without borders and nations, the individual is left depending completely on himself, without protecting associations (or power-limiting entities and bonds), completely at the mercy and disposal of a new, globally extended system of power.

Judging by the experience of history, however, the creation of a single, unified and universal civilization (seen by Spengler as the ultimate stage of any high cultural formation) has always gone hand in hand with the absolute universal rule of an imperial bureaucracy over subjects who no longer saw themselves as citizens or members of any specific nation, but as human beings and members of the human race. Since the first century A.D., the Roman civilization spread around the Mediterranean basin and environs, and the same amphitheaters, aqueducts, bathing cultures, military fortifications and urban planning concepts could be found anywhere from Britain and Germany down to Italy and Asia Minor. Yet in those days, absolute power was exercised as well over subjects without political rights, for the sake of universal peace and the "salus generis humani." (The same spirit can be found in the ultimate stages of all the high cultures, when one autocratic ruler finally governed over one unified, universal civilization — from the empires of Mesopotamia, Egypt and China down to the reign of Moctezuma II over the highly civilized and culturally advanced empire of the Aztecs with its monumental, highly organized and regulated imperial city of Tenochtitlan). Perhaps similarly, the emergence of one unified globalized culture with the same U.S.-inspired movies, entertainment, music, shopping habits, ways of life, business concepts and financial market language extending almost anywhere across the civilized world provides early indications in the early years of the 21st century that the superpower may one day assume political responsibility as well and proceed towards the establishment of one universal, imperial power structure.

Judging by historical experience and analogy, the one world with one humankind, one culture, one race and eternal, everlasting peace, which is so desired today by progressive intellectual forces in the West, may point towards the establishment not of a free, liberal world republic but rather of a global, peace-preserving empire governed by supreme, absolute rule.

LIST OF REFERENCES

Adler, Eric, "Post 9/11 Views of Rome and the Nature of 'Defensive Imperialism'," in: *International Journal of the Classical Tradition*, 15 (2008), 587-610.

Arendt, Hannah, *The Human Condition*, London and Chicago 1958.

Arendt, Hannah, *On Revolution*, London 1990.

Arendt, Hannah, *The Origins of Totalitarianism*, New York 1951.

Aubert, Jean-Jacques, "The Republican Economy and Roman Law. Regulation, Promotion, or Reflection?," in: Flower (ed.), 160-178.

Bacevich, Andrew C. (ed.), *The Imperial Tense. Problems and Prospects of American Empire*, Chicago 2003.

Badian, E., *Roman Imperialism in the Late Republic*, Oxford 1968.

Bageant, Joe, *Deer Hunting with Jesus. Dispatches from America's Class War*, New York 2007.

Beard, Mary / Crawford, Michael, *Rome in the Late Republic: Problems and Interpretations*, London 1999.

Beck, Hans, *Polis und Koinon. Untersuchungen zur Geschichte und Struktur der griechischen Bundesstaaten im 4. Jahrhundert vor Christus*, Stuttgart 1997.

Bello, Walden, *The Dilemma of Domination. The Unmaking of the American Empire*, New York 2005.

Bender, Peter, "The New Rome," in: Andrew C. Bacevich (ed.), *The Imperial Tense. Problems and Prospects of American Empire*, Chicago 2003, 81-92.

Bender, Peter, *Weltmacht Amerika. Das neue Rom*, Munich 2005.

Boardman, John / Griffin, Jasper / Murray, Oswyn (eds.), *The Oxford History of the Roman World*, Oxford 1991.

Boot, Max, "Plädoyer für ein Empire," in: Speck, Ulrich / Sznaider, Natan (eds.), *Empire Amerika. Perspektiven einer neuen Weltordnung*, Munich 2003, 60-70.

Branham, Robert Bracht / Goulet-Cazé, Marie-Odile (eds.), *The Cynics. The Cynic Movement in Antiquity and its Legacy*, Berkeley et al. 1996.

Bringmann, Klaus, *Krise und Ende der römischen Republik (133-42 v. Chr.)*, Berlin 2003.

Brunt, Peter A., *The Fall of the Roman Republic and related essays*, Oxford 1988.

Bugh, Glenn R. (ed.), *The Cambridge Companion to the Hellenistic World*, Cambridge/Mass. 2006.

Chamoux, François, *Hellenistic Civilisation*, Oxford 2003.

Christ, Karl, *Das Römische Weltreich. Aufstieg und Zerfall einer antiken Großmacht*, Freiburg/Basel/Wien 1973.

Chua, Amy, *Day of Empire. How Superpowers Rise to Global Dominance and Why They Fall*, New York 2007.

Cox, Michael, "Empire? The Bush Doctrine and the Lessons of History," in: David Held / Mathias Koenig-Archibuge (eds.), *American Power in the Twenty-First Century*, Malden/Mass. 2004, 21-51.

Debray, Regis, *Empire 2.0. A Modest Proposal for a United States of the West*, Berkeley 2004.

Eckstein, Arthur M., "Rome and the Hellenistic World: Masculinity and Militarism, Monarchy and Republic," in: Tabachnick, David / Koivukoski, Toivo (eds.), *Enduring Empire. Ancient Lessons for Global Politics*, Toronto 2009, 114-126.

Errington, R. Malcolm, *A History of the Hellenistic World, 323–30 B.C.*, Malden/Mass 2008.

Erskine, Andrew, *The Hellenistic Stoa. Political Thought and Action*, London 1990.

Ferguson, Niall, *Colossus. The Rise and Fall of the American Empire*, London 2004.

Flower, Harriet E. (ed.), *The Cambridge Companion to the Roman Republic*, Cambridge 2004.

Forte, Betty, *Rome and the Romans how the Greeks saw them*, Rome 1972.

Fox, Robin Lane, *Alexander the Great*, London 1973.

Frank, Thomas, *Pity the Billionaire. The Hard-Times Swindle and the Unlikely Comeback of the Right*, New York 2012.

Fukuyama, Francis, *America at the Crossroads. Democracy, Power and the Neoconservative Legacy*, New Haven 2006.

Goulet-Cazé, Marie-Odile, "Religion and the Early Cynics," in: Branham/Goulet-Cazé (eds.), 47-80.

Gruen, E.S., *The Hellenistic World and the Coming of Rome*, 2 volumes, Berkeley 1984.

Hedges, Chris, *Death of the Liberal Class*, New York 2010.

Hedges, Chris, *The Empire of Illusion. The End of Literacy and the Triumph of Spectacle*, New York 2009.

Hendrickson, David Edward, "In the Mirror of Antiquity: The Problem of American Empire," in Tabachnick/Koivukoski (eds.), 3-19.

Ignatieff, Michael, *Empire Lite, Nation-Building in Bosnia, Kosovo and Afghanistan*, Toronto 2003.

Ikenberry, G. John, "American Power and the Empire of Capitalist Democracy," in: Michael Cox et al. (eds.), *Empires, Systems and States. Great Transformations in International Politics*, Cambridge 2001, 191-212.

Immermann, Richard H., *Empire for Liberty. A History of American Imperialism from Benjamin Franklin to Paul Wolfowitz*, Princeton/New York/Oxford 2010.

Johnson, Chalmers. *Nemesis. The Last Days of the American Republic*, New York 2006.

Johnson, Chalmers, *The Sorrows of Empire. Militarism, Secrecy and the End of the Republic*, New York 2004.

Johnson, Simon, *13 Bankers. The Wallstreet Takeover and the Next Financial Meltdown*, New York 2011.

Kagan, Robert, *Of Paradise and Power. America and Europe in the New World Order*, New York 2003.

Kallet-Marx, Robert, *Hegemony to Empire. The Development of the Roman Imperium in the East from 148 to 62 B.C.*, Berkeley 1995.

Kaplan, Robert, *Warrior Politics. Why Leadership Demands a Pagan Ethos*, New York 2002.

Kennedy, Paul, *The Rise and Fall of the Great Powers. Economic Change and Military Conflict from 1500 to 2000*, New York 1987.

Kissinger, Henry, *Does America Need a Foreign Policy. Toward a New Diplomacy for the 21st Century*, New York 2001.

Klauck, Hans-Josef, *The Religious Context of Early Christianity. A Guide to Greco–Roman Religions*, London/New York 2003.

Krevens, Nita / Sens, Alexander, "Language and Literature," in: Bugh (ed.), 186-207.

Kupchan, Charles A., *The End of the American Era. U.S. Foreign Policy and the Geopolitics of the Twenty-First Century*, New York 2002.

Laqueur, Walter, *After the Fall. The End of the European Dream and the Decline of a Continent*, New York 2012.

Larsen, A.O., *Greek Federal States. Their Institutions and History*, Oxford 1968.

Long, A.A., *From Epicurus to Epictetus. Studies in Hellenistic and Roman Philosophy*, Oxford/New York 2006.

Long, A.A., "The Socratic Tradition. Diogenes, Crates and Hellenistic Ethics," in: Branham/Goulet-Cazé (eds.), 28-46.

Long, A.A./ Sedley, D.N., *The Hellenistic Philosophers* (German version), Stuttgart/Weimar 2000.

Lord, Cames, *Proconsuls. Delegated Political-Military Leadership from Rome to America Today*, New York 2012.

Madden, Thomas F., *Empires of Trust. How Rome Built — and America is Building — A New World*, New York 2008.

Malamud, Margaret, *Ancient Rome and Modern America*, Oxford 2008.

Marquand, David, "Playground Bully," in: Bacevich (ed.), 111-118.

Mikalson, Jon D., "Greek Religion. Continuity and Change in the Hellenistic Period," in: Bugh (ed.), 208-222.

Moles, John L., "Cynic Cosmopolitanism," in: Branham/Goulet-Cazé (eds.), 105-120.

Mossé, Claude, *Athens in Decline 404-86 B.C.* (German edition), Munich/Zurich 1979.

Murphy, Cullen, *Are We Rome? The Fall of an Empire and the Fate of America*, Boston/New York 2008.

Myers, Miner, *Liberty without Anarchy. A History of the Society of the Cincinnati*, Charlottesville 1983.

Orlin, Eric, "Urban Religion in the Middle and Late Republic," in: Rüpke, Jörg (ed.), *A Companion to Roman Religion*, Malden/Mass 2007, 58-70.

Packer, George, *The Unwinding. An Inner History of the New America*, New York 2013.

Pearson, Monte L., *Perils of Empire. The Roman Republic and the American Republic*, New York 2008.

Potter, David, "The Roman Army and Navy," in: Flower (ed.), 66-88.

Rüpke, Jörg, "Roman Religion," in: Flower (ed.), 179-195.

Scahill, Jeremy, *Blackwater. The Rise of the World's Most Powerful Mercenary Army*, London 2007.

Schama, Simon, "The Unloved American. Two Centuries of Alienating Europe," in: *The New Yorker*, 10 March 2003.

Schlesinger, Arthur M., *The Imperial Presidency* (With a New Introduction), New York 2004.

Schulten, A., "Roman Cruelty and Extortion," in: Erich Gruen (ed.). *Imperialism in the Roman Republic*, New York 1970, 60-66.

Sellers, Mortimer N.S., *American Republicans. Roman Ideology in the United States Constitution*, Basingstoke/New York 1994.

Sharples, Robert W., "Philosophy for Life," in: Bugh (ed.), 223-240.

Sharples, Robert W., *Stoics, Epicureans and Skeptics. An Introduction to Hellenistic Philosophy*, New York 1996.

Shipley, Graham, *The Greek World after Alexander, 323-30 B.C.* London/ New York 2000.

Spengler, Oswald, *Der Untergang des Abendlandes. Umrisse einer Morphologie der Weltgeschichte*, Munich 1963.

Stieglitz, Joseph, *Price of Inequality. How Today's Divided Society Endangers Our Future*, New York 2012.

Stockton, David, *Cicero. A Political Biography*, Oxford 1971.

Stone, Oliver / Kuznick, Peter, *The Concise Untold History of the United States*, London 2014.

Thompson, Dorothy J., "The Hellenistic Family," in: Bugh (ed.), 93-112.

Todd, Emmanuel, *After the Empire. The Breakdown of the American Order*, New York 2003.

van Bremen, R., "Woman and Wealth," in: Cameron. A./Kuhrt, A. (eds.), *Images of Women in Antiquity*, London 1993.

Varoufakis, Yanis, *The Global Minotaur. America, Europe and the Future of the Global Economy*, New York 2013.

von Ungern-Sternberg, Jürgen, "The Crisis of the Republic," in: Flower (ed.), 89-109.

Walbank, Frank William, *The Hellenistic World* (German edition), Munich 1983.

Winter, Rolf, *Ami Go Home. Plädoyer für den Abschied von einem gewalttätigen Land*, Hamburg 1989.

Wyke, Maria, "A Twenty-First Century Caesar," in: Wyke, Maria (ed.), *Julius Caesar in Western Culture*, Malden/Mass. 2006, 305-323.

Index

Printed in the United States
By Bookmasters